ECONOMIC ISSUES, PROBLEMS AND PERSPECTIVES

FEDERAL EXCISE TAXES

ELEMENTS AND SELECT ANALYSES

Economic Issues, Problems and Perspectives

Additional books in this series can be found on Nova's website under the Series tab.

Additional E-books in this series can be found on Nova's website under the E-book tab.

ECONOMIC ISSUES, PROBLEMS AND PERSPECTIVES

FEDERAL EXCISE TAXES

ELEMENTS AND SELECT ANALYSES

JEROLD M. BUSCH
EDITOR

NOVINKA
New York

For permission to use material from this book please contact us:
Telephone 631-231-7269; Fax 631-231-8175
Web Site: http://www.novapublishers.com

Additional color graphics may be available in the e-book version of this book.

Library of Congress Cataloging-in-Publication Data

ISBN: 978-1-62948-483-9

Published by Nova Science Publishers, Inc. † New York

CONTENTS

PREFACE

There are four common types of excise taxes: (1) sumptuary (or "sin") taxes, (2) regulatory or environmental taxes, (3) benefit-based taxes (or user charges), and (4) luxury taxes. Sumptuary taxes were traditionally imposed for moral reasons, but are currently rationalized, in part, to discourage a specific activity that is thought to have negative spillover effects (or "externalities") on society. Regulatory or environmental taxes are imposed to offset external costs associated with regulating public safety or to discourage consumption of a specific commodity that is thought to have negative externalities on society. Benefit-based taxes (which include user charges) are imposed to charge users of a particular public good for financing and maintenance of that public good. Lastly, luxury taxes are primarily imposed as one way to raise revenue, particularly from higher-income households.

This bookprovides an introduction and general analysis of excise taxes. First, a brief history of U.S. excise tax policy is provided. Second, the various forms of excise taxes and their respective administrative advantages and disadvantages are described. Third, the effect of federal excise taxes on federal, state, and local tax revenue is discussed. Fourth, the economic effects of various types of excise taxes are analyzed. The effects on consumer behavior and equity among taxpayers could be important issues for assessment of current excise tax policy or for the design of new excise taxes.

Chapter 1 - Excise taxes have generally played a diminishing role in financing the federal government since the middle of the 20th century for multiple reasons. First, Congress has taken legislative action to eliminate many categories of excise taxes. Second, most excise tax rates set in statute have declined in value over time due to inflation and inaction by Congress to change tax rates set in statute.

Excise taxes tend to be regressive, in that lower-income households generally pay a larger share of their income in excise taxes than higher-income households. Because excise taxes generally increase the price of the taxed commodity, they also tend to lower consumer demand.

Excise taxes play a much smaller role in financing the federal government than they did in the past. In 1960, federal excise tax collections were $355.49 billion (in 2012 constant dollars, after accounting for inflation). In FY2012, federal excise tax collections were $56.17 billion (roughly one-sixth of their 1960 value in 2012 constant dollars). Federal excise taxes comprised 7.0% of all federal revenue in 1973, whereas they comprised 3.2% in 2012.

Congress may be interested in revisiting the revenue and economic effects of excise taxes because these taxes could play a growing role in financing public goods. Some long-standing excise tax proposals to correct alleged social costs have resurfaced from time to time in policy discussions. Some of these proposals could be targeted towards specific products or activities (e.g., a "sugar-sweetened beverages" tax), while others could affect a broad range of economic activity and raise a significant amount of revenue (e.g., a carbon tax). On the other hand, there is also interest in reducing current excise tax rates as a means to encourage short-term growth in particular industries.

Chapter 2 – As a result of the recent debate over guns, gun rights, and gun-related violence, there has been a marked increase in sales of many weapons as well as ammunition. Through an excise tax on firearms and ammunition, such sales have a marked beneficial effect on funding for state wildlife programs through the Wildlife Restoration Program (also known as Pittman-Robertson or P-R). This report examines these taxes, their allocation, and their use. It also examines the effects of sequestration of this account, pursuant to the Budget Control Act of 2011 (BCA; P.L. 112-25).

Chapter 3 – On December 7, 2012, the Department of the Treasury and the Internal Revenue Service issued final regulations explaining the scope of the medical device excise tax created by the Health Care and Education Reconciliation Act of 2010 (HCERA), which modified the Patient Protection and Affordable Care Act of 2010. The new regulations were issued less than a month before the 2.3% excise tax took effect on January 1, 2013. This report provides a brief overview of the recently enacted Treasury regulations and the legal implications of the regulations.

The Treasury regulations on the medical device excise tax explain both who is subject to the excise tax and the scope of the statutory exemptions provided for the tax. Specifically, the regulations incorporate by reference the general definitions for a "manufacturer, producer, or importer" outlined in the

Internal Revenue Code, meaning that the excise tax will be directly paid by manufacturers, as opposed to consumers or others that use a given medical device.

Furthermore, the regulations attempt to clarify the limits to the medical device excise tax. Beyond the statutory exemptions created for eyeglasses, contact lenses, and hearing aids, the law created a "retail exemption" to the excise tax, excluding from the tax medical devices that are "generally purchased by the general public at retail for individual use." The Treasury regulations attempt to simultaneously provide certainty to potential taxpayers as to which devices are subject to the retail exemption, while allowing the government the flexibility to properly apply the retail exemption to the variety of devices that could be exposed to the excise tax. The regulations provide a flexible two-prong test to determine whether a device should fall within the retail exemption, applying the exemption when the device is (1) regularly available for purchase by non-professional consumers and (2) not primarily intended for use by medical professionals. The regulations provide several factors to consider when applying the two-prong test. To provide some certainty to the scope of the retail exemption, the regulations also included several "safe harbor" provisions, explicitly acknowledging that certain devices, such as "over-the-counter" devices, fall within the retail exemption.

The new Treasury regulations on the medical device excise tax, while providing some certainty with respect to what devices will be exempt from the tax, generally favor a more flexible approach to defining the scope of the central exemption to the tax. As a consequence, uncertainty remains as to which medical devices will be subject to the tax. Indeed, Treasury, in releasing the medical device excise tax regulations, notes that further clarification on various issues implicated by the tax is still needed. As such, the regulations constitute only the first step in defining the limits of the medical device excise tax.

Chapter 4 – Excise taxes have long been a part of our country's revenue history. In the field of gasoline taxation, the states led the way with Oregon enacting the first tax on motor fuels in 1919. By 1932, all states and the District of Columbia had followed suit with tax rates that ranged between two and seven cents per gallon. The federal government first imposed its excise tax on gasoline at a one-cent per gallon rate in 1932. The gas tax was enacted to correct a federal budgetary imbalance. It continued to support general revenue during World War II and the Korean War.

Economists know the gasoline excise tax as a "manufacturer's excise tax" because the government imposes it at production (i.e., the producer, refiner, or importer) for efficiency in collection. Particularly in the short run, when the demand for gasoline is relatively inelastic, economists recognize that any increase in the gasoline tax ultimately falls on the consumer.

The *Highway Revenue Act of 1956* established the federal Highway Trust Fund (HTF) for the direct purpose of funding the construction of an interstate highway system, and aiding in the finance of primary, secondary, and urban routes. Each time Congress has extended the Highway Trust Fund it has also extended the federal excise tax on gasoline.

In the 112th Congress, a series of extensions of the surface transportation legislation have occurred. These extensions reauthorized the federal government's highway, mass transit, and surface transportation safety programs and levied highway user taxes. Extended taxes on gasoline and diesel fuels provided approximately 90% of the funding for the Highway Trust Fund and 80% of the funding for mass transit programs. Other extended taxes were levied on heavy trucks, truck tires, gasohol, and fuel from natural or petroleum gas.

On March 4, 2011, President Obama signed H.R. 662, the *Surface Transportation Extension Act of 2011* (P.L. 112-5). This law extended federal-aid highway, highway safety, motor carrier safety transit, and other programs funded out of the Highway Trust Fund through September 30, 2011. On September 16, 2011, President Obama signed H.R. 2887, *Surface and Air Transportation Programs Extension Act of 2011* (P.L. 112-30), which extended, through March 31, 2012, current surface transportation programs and the motor fuel, heavy truck, and truck tire taxes that support the HTF. On March 30, 2012, President Obama signed H.R. 4281, *Surface Transportation Extension Act of 2012* (P.L. 112-102), which extended the federal surface transportation programs and financing through June 30, 2012. On June 29, 2012, President Obama signed H.R. 6064, *Temporary Surface Transportation Extension Act of 2012* (P.L. 112-140), which extended the surface transportation programs and financing through July 6, 2012. On July 6, 2012, President Obama signed H.R. 4348, *Moving Ahead for Progress in the 21st Century Act* or *Map-21* (P.L. 112-141). This law authorized appropriations for the federal surface transportation programs through October 1, 2014, and financing, including gasoline and diesel taxes, through September 30, 2016. The extended gasoline tax rate was 18.4 cents per gallon and the extended diesel tax rate was 24.4 cents per gallon. These rates include a 0.1 cent per gallon tax levied and deposited in the Leaking Underground Storage Tank (LUST) Trust Fund.

Chapter 5 – Under current law, the excise tax on rum is $13.50 per proof gallon and is collected on rum produced in or imported into the United States. Through 2011, $13.25 per proof gallon of imported rum is transferred or "covered over" to the Treasuries of Puerto Rico (PR) and the United States Virgin Islands (USVI). In FY2011, PR received over $449.0 million in revenue and the USVI received over $133.5 million. The law does not impose any restrictions on how PR and USVI can use the transferred revenues. Both territories use some portion of the revenue to promote and assist the rum industry.

The cover-over provisions for rum extend as far back as 1917 for PR and 1954 for USVI. Recently, the United States Virgin Islands has dedicated a larger share of current and future covered-over revenue to help finance public and private infrastructure that would directly benefit the rum industry.

In the 112th Congress, legislation has been introduced to expand federal control over the use of covered-over revenue. Passage of H.R. 1883 (or similar legislation, S. 986) would result in limits on Puerto Rico's and the USVI's ability to use covered-over revenue to subsidize the rum industry in the islands. The legislation is likely in response to the recent economic development initiatives in the USVI financed in part by rum cover-over revenue. The President's FY2013 budget proposal includes an extension of the $13.25 cover-over, as does S. 3521.

This report provides a history and analysis of the rum cover-over program and current legislative efforts to modify the program. The congressional debate on this legislation could also lead to debate on the broader issue of the cover-over program more generally.

In: Federal Excise Taxes
Editor: Jerold M. Busch

ISBN: 978-1-62948-483-9

Chapter 1

FEDERAL EXCISE TAXES: AN INTRODUCTION AND GENERAL ANALYSIS*

Sean Lowry

SUMMARY

There are four common types of excise taxes: (1) sumptuary (or "sin") taxes, (2) regulatory or environmental taxes, (3) benefit-based taxes (or user charges), and (4) luxury taxes. Sumptuary taxes were traditionally imposed for moral reasons, but are currently rationalized, in part, to discourage a specific activity that is thought to have negative spillover effects (or "externalities") on society. Regulatory or environmental taxes are imposed to offset external costs associated with regulating public safety or to discourage consumption of a specific commodity that is thought to have negative externalities on society. Benefit-based taxes (which include user charges) are imposed to charge users of a particular public good for financing and maintenance of that public good. Lastly, luxury taxes are primarily imposed as one way to raise revenue, particularly from higher-income households.

This report provides an introduction and general analysis of excise taxes. First, a brief history of U.S. excise tax policy is provided. Second, the various forms of excise taxes and their respective administrative

---

* This is an edited, reformatted and augmented version of Congressional Research Service, Publication No. R43189, dated August 26, 2013.

advantages and disadvantages are described. Third, the effect of federal excise taxes on federal, state, and local tax revenue is discussed. Fourth, the economic effects of various types of excise taxes are analyzed. The effects on consumer behavior and equity among taxpayers could be important issues for assessment of current excise tax policy or for the design of new excise taxes.

Excise taxes have generally played a diminishing role in financing the federal government since the middle of the 20th century for multiple reasons. First, Congress has taken legislative action to eliminate many categories of excise taxes. Second, most excise tax rates set in statute have declined in value over time due to inflation and inaction by Congress to change tax rates set in statute.

Excise taxes tend to be regressive, in that lower-income households generally pay a larger share of their income in excise taxes than higher-income households. Because excise taxes generally increase the price of the taxed commodity, they also tend to lower consumer demand.

Excise taxes play a much smaller role in financing the federal government than they did in the past. In 1960, federal excise tax collections were $355.49 billion (in 2012 constant dollars, after accounting for inflation). In FY2012, federal excise tax collections were $56.17 billion (roughly one-sixth of their 1960 value in 2012 constant dollars). Federal excise taxes comprised 7.0% of all federal revenue in 1973, whereas they comprised 3.2% in 2012.

Congress may be interested in revisiting the revenue and economic effects of excise taxes because these taxes could play a growing role in financing public goods. Some long-standing excise tax proposals to correct alleged social costs have resurfaced from time to time in policy discussions. Some of these proposals could be targeted towards specific products or activities (e.g., a “sugar-sweetened beverages” tax), while others could affect a broad range of economic activity and raise a significant amount of revenue (e.g., a carbon tax). On the other hand, there is also interest in reducing current excise tax rates as a means to encourage short-term growth in particular industries.

INTRODUCTION

Excise taxes are selective taxes on specific forms of consumption or behavior (compared to general sales taxes which tend to apply to all forms of consumption, with some exceptions). Today, federal excise taxes apply to a wide variety of consumer goods and economic activities, such as alcohol, tobacco, firearms and ammunition, gasoline, the industrial use of ozone-depleting chemicals, and indoor tanning services.

There are four common purposes of excise taxes: (1) sumptuary (or “sin”) taxes, (2) regulatory or environmental taxes, (3) benefit-based taxes (or user charges), and (4) luxury taxes.[1] Sumptuary (or “sin”) taxes were traditionally imposed for moral reasons, but are currently rationalized, in part, to discourage a specific activity that is thought to have negative spillover effects (or “externalities”) on society.[2] Generally, sumptuary taxes in the United States refer to excise taxes on alcohol or tobacco consumption. Regulatory or environmental taxes are imposed to offset for external costs associated with regulating public safety or to discourage consumption of a specific commodity that is thought to have negative externalities on society. Benefit-based taxes are imposed to charge users for the benefits received from a particular public good and are often used for maintenance and upkeep of that public good. Lastly, luxury taxes are primarily imposed as one way to raise revenue, particularly from higher-income households.[3]

The role of excise taxes has changed over time. Excise taxes narrowly imposed on the consumption of certain products, such as alcohol and tobacco, formed the basis for much of federal tax revenue until the modern income tax was enacted in the early 20th century. Although excise taxes have played a diminishing role in the mix of federal revenue sources over time, there has been persistent interest in the possible use of excise taxes to raise revenue or provide disincentives to behavior that is believed by some to have negative effects on society (e.g., a tax on carbon emissions). On the other hand, there is also interest in reducing current excise tax rates as a means to encourage short-term growth in particular industries.[4]

This report provides an introduction and general analysis of excise taxes. First, a brief history of the role of excise taxes is provided.

Second, the various forms of excise taxes and their respective administrative advantages and disadvantages are described.

Third, the effect of federal excise taxes on federal, state, and local tax revenue is discussed. Fourth, the economic effects of various types of excise taxes are analyzed. The effects on consumer behavior and equity among taxpayers could be important issues for assessment of current excise tax policy or for the design of new excise taxes.

Lastly, the **Appendix** to this report contains a list of references to other CRS reports on specific excise taxes.[5]

Historical Summary of Federal Excise Taxes

Federal excise taxes have had a dynamic role within the U.S. tax system. The history of the federal excise tax system is often one that coincides with wars, serving as an emergency source of funds, or reflects periodic concerns about rising budget deficits.[6] Except for taxes on tobacco and liquor, new excise taxes seem to have been used extensively for the control of social costs and as user charges in recent years.

Excise taxes played a key fiscal role in the early history of the United States.[7] The federal government initially relied on customs duties (tariffs) on foreign trade. In 1791, during the presidency of George Washington, Secretary of the Treasury Alexander Hamilton implemented the first federal excise tax on whiskey. The whiskey tax was used as a means to fund the fledgling federal government, repay debts from the American Revolution, and help to establish federal supremacy over the states.[8] The burden of the tax was controversial along geographic divisions (Westerners on the frontier tended to both consume more whiskey and use it as a medium of financial exchange) and ideological divisions (Federalists versus Anti-Federalists). This opposition peaked in the famous “Whiskey Rebellion” of 1794 in southwestern Pennsylvania, where President Washington led 13,000 troops to suppress an armed rebellion. After the suppression of the Whiskey Rebellion in 1794, Congress passed excise taxes on tobacco, snuff tobacco, sugar, and carriages.[9] In 1797, a direct tax was imposed on the ownership of houses, land, and slaves as tariff revenue declined during a period when European powers were engaged in war (with the United States sided against France). The unpopularity of the taxes contributed to Thomas Jefferson’s defeat of Federalist Party candidate John Adams during the presidential election of 1800. All internal excise taxes were repealed in 1802, as the fiscal demand arising from the war in Europe abated.[10]

Federal excise taxes continued to play a significant role in public finances throughout the 1800s. Excises were temporarily reintroduced during the War of 1812, but were repealed from 1817 until the Civil War.[11] Following the onset of the Civil War, Congress passed the Revenue Act of 1861, which restored earlier excise taxes.[12] Most of these excise taxes were repealed after the end of the Civil War, with taxes on distilled spirits and tobacco remaining in effect. In the decades after the Civil War, excise taxes accounted for between one-third and one-half of all federal revenue.[13] Excises were the single largest source of internal revenue during this era.[14] During the Spanish-American War (1898), excise tax revenue was a larger source of federal tax collections than even customs duties on foreign imports, as revenue from tariffs tended to decline during wartime. Emergency excise taxes were levied on a variety of items to fund military spending during the Spanish-American War, such as pianos, playing cards, yachts, and billiard tables. After the end of the war most of these emergency excise taxes were repealed.

Excise taxes were utilized to fund war-time spending during the early 20th century. Temporary excise tax provisions were imposed in the Revenue Act of 1918, passed during World War I, to help fund war-time spending, including the first excise tax on firearms, shells, and cartridges. As a result, excise tax collections quadrupled from 1914 to 1919.[15] Excise tax revenues declined significantly after the beginning of Prohibition (falling to less than half of the pre-Prohibition revenue levels by 1930) but rebounded above the pre-Prohibition levels after the consumption of alcohol was made legal again after 1933.[16] Existing excise tax rates were increased again virtually across-the-board around the time of World War II, and new taxes on luxury goods (such as toiletries and furs) were introduced.[17] Additionally, Congress rejected adopting a general sales tax twice during this era (1932 and 1942), despite critiques that the costs of administering excises to a growing list of products was high and the revenue gained from many excises was small.[18]

Excise taxes underwent a time of dynamic reform during the latter half of the 20th century. The Revenue Act of 1951 increased many excise tax rates in existence at the time (such as alcohol and tobacco) and increased the tax base for some user charges. However, the Excise Tax Reduction Act of 1954 (P.L. 83-324) and the Excise Tax Reduction Act of 1965 (P.L. 89-44) reduced the number of provisions and their respective tax rates. In particular, the Excise Tax Reduction Act of 1965 eliminated most federal excise taxes with the goal being to "help sustain economic expansion."[19]

Certain excise taxes were also expanded, in part, to reflect a desire for a wider role for the federal government. An example of this linkage between excise taxes and the expansion of federally provided public goods would be the modern highway system.[20] The Highway Revenue Act of 1956 (P.L. 84-627) increased the federal gasoline tax (in effect since 1932) and directed its collections from the Treasury's General Fund specifically towards funding of public highways.[21] Specific excise taxes linked to trust funds related to air travel, mining, waterway travel, oil spills, and other hazardous chemicals (among others) were created in the 1970s and 1980s. A rising budget deficit helped to bring about the excise tax increases in the Omnibus Budget Reconciliation Act of 1990 (OBRA90; P.L. 101-508). OBRA90 increased tax rates on distilled spirits (last increased in 1985), beer and wine (last increased in 1951), tobacco (last increased in 1982), and gasoline (last increased in 1982).

Since 2000, excise taxes have played a diminishing role in the mix of federal revenue sources even as new provisions have been introduced. As discussed later in the "Revenue" section of this report, excise tax collections have increased in nominal amounts, but have decreased in inflation-adjusted (real) values and as a share of overall federal revenue. The rates on major excise taxes have remained unadjusted for inflation for years, such as the excise taxes on gasoline (since 1997) and alcohol (1991). The excise tax on tobacco was last increased with the Children's Health Insurance Program Reauthorization Act of 2009 (P.L. 111-3), but revenue from the tobacco tax has declined over time in part due to decreased demand for tobacco products.

Recently, new excise taxes have been introduced. Several new excise taxes were created by the Patient Protection and Affordable Care Act (P.L. 111-148 and P.L. 111-152, as amended), such as taxes on indoor tanning bed services, medical devices, and certain high-value insurance plans.

The future role of federal excise taxes in federal policy is still unclear. Excise taxes in the form of user charges could continue to play a role in financing public goods and services. Excises could be one tool to raise revenue, particularly in the absence of a general consumption tax at the federal level.[22] Some long-standing excise tax proposals to correct a perceived social issue have also resurfaced in policy discussions. Some of these proposals could be targeted towards specific products or activities (e.g., a "sugar-sweetened beverages" tax), while others could affect a broad range of economic activity and raise a significant amount of revenue (e.g., a carbon tax).[23]

ADMINISTRATION

All forms of excise tax use some sort of physical control or measurement by the excise authorities to determine tax liability and ensure compliance with the law.[24] This section of the report describes the different ways that excise taxes are structured, and the advantages and disadvantages of each model.

Setting the Tax Rate

For excise taxes intended to compensate for the social costs of certain activities, economic theory suggests that the excise tax rate should be set at a level that offsets the negative costs of that consumption to society.[25]

In general, an excise tax rate can be applied in one of two ways:

- *Per unit*: where the tax rate is applied per individual unit produced, purchased, or sold. For example, different per-unit rates are levied on tobacco products based on the product type: 1,000 units of cigarettes or one pound of pipe tobacco.
- *Ad valorem*: where the tax rate is applied as a percentage of the value of the product, either based on the manufacturer's, wholesale, or retail price. For example, the excise tax on firearms and ammunition is set at 10% of the wholesale price for pistols and revolvers, and 11% for other firearms as well as shells or cartridges.[26]

Economists say that per-unit excise taxes are more appropriate when marginal consumption of the targeted commodity is allegedly deleterious. For example, cigarette taxes are levied per unit sold because the alleged spillover effects of smoking (e.g., second-hand smoking) occur with every pack of cigarettes smoked. The excise tax on gasoline is levied per gallon of gasoline sold because the amount of gasoline consumed was a rough approximation of how much driving one did, and thus how much wear and tear a driver would impose on federally managed highways.

However, arguments can be made against these justifications for per unit taxes. Per-unit taxes can invite issues of both horizontal and vertical equality (as addressed later in this report). Also, because per-unit taxes are often set at static rates in statute, these rates often fall in inflation-adjusted (or "real") terms.[27] For example, the statutory federal excise tax rate on distilled spirits in 1951 was set to $10.50 per proof gallon (ppg).[28] Legislation was passed in 1985 increasing the statutory tax rate from $10.50 to $12.50 ppg, and again in 1990 increasing the tax rate from $12.50 to $13.50 ppg. The excise tax rate on distilled spirits still remains at the 1990 level of $13.50 ppg, or $2.14 per 750ml bottle (a "fifth") of 80-proof liquor.[29] If the 1951 tax rate was indexed for inflation, it would be over $95.65 ppg in 2013 dollars, or approximately $19.49 per 750 ml bottle of 80 proof liquor.[30]

In contrast, *ad valorem* tax rates largely avoid a real decline in value because they are applied based on the price of commodity or activity rather than the quantity consumed or produced. *Ad valorem* rates can also be more progressive than per-unit rates especially if the commodity taxed is a luxury good (whereby demand increases more than proportionally as income rises). However, *ad valorem* rates also have the capability to be regressive if the consumers of the commodity are not limited to those at the upper end of the income distribution.

Choosing the Stage of Production to Levy the Tax

An excise tax can also be levied at different stages along a commodity's production and distribution chain:[31]

- Production level: collected on sales by producers to wholesalers, retailers, or other producers. Transactions prior to the sale by the last producer are often partially exempted or taxed at reduced rates.
- Manufacturing level: collected on sales by manufacturers to wholesalers or retailers, including occasional direct sales to consumers.
- Wholesale level: collected on sales by the last wholesaler or manufacturer to retailers, including occasional direct sales to consumers.
- Retail level: collected on sales by retailers to final consumer, including wholesalers or manufacturers selling occasionally to consumers.
- Turnover taxes: collected on sales at all or nearly all stages, and also known as "cascade taxes" on account of their cumulative effects.

Generally, an excise tax that is levied at earlier stages in the production process has lower administrative costs and fewer opportunities for tax evasion. In most situations, consumers vastly outnumber producers. Trying to implement an excise tax at the level of the consumer retail outlet results often in a duplication of bureaucratic processes compared to a tax on manufacturers. For example, more than 303 billion cigarettes were purchased across the United States in 2010, but 85% of these cigarettes were manufactured by three companies.[32] However, *ad valorem* taxes imposed at the manufacturer's level could provide an incentive for value-added options to be ordered further down the supply chain in an attempt to minimize the tax burden. For example, the manufacturer tax on firearms is levied on the assembly of a complete rifle, but any add-ons or modification kits to that rifle are not taxed.[33]

Taxes imposed at the manufacturing level could lead to an effective tax rate that is higher than the statutory tax rate. This outcome occurs because some manufactured goods have a long inventory life, and a considerable time period may elapse between when the tax is paid (when the good leaves the manufacturer's premises) and the date that the good is sold. In effect, the manufacturer incurs an interest cost to borrow the money to pay the tax.[34]

The advantage of imposing a tax at the retail level is that it can more easily exclude certain consumers from an excise tax's revenue base, if desired. For example, farmers can receive an excise tax credit for certain fuel purchased for farm use, as this activity generally has a minimal effect on the quality of interstate highways.[35] On the other hand, exemptions could diminish the effect of the tax on the original goal of the tax. An exemption, in the form of a refund, can be implemented through a manufacturer's tax, although this might require additional administrative resources.

Transition Issues

Special rules are sometimes used to accompany the imposition of a new excise tax or increases in any existing tax rates to prevent tax avoidance. If an excise tax is announced effective as of a specific date in the future, then individuals might stockpile the taxed commodity. One policy to prevent this behavior is a "floor stocks" tax, or an excise tax on all existing inventory as of a particular date. The floor stocks tax is usually imposed on the date a new tax takes effect or the date after a tax-rate increase takes effect; all new inventory subject to tax that is acquired after the new tax becomes effective is then subject to the new tax.

Excise Tax Reporting

Tax liability for most federal excise taxes is reported on IRS Form 720 "Quarterly Federal Excise Tax Return." This form is generally due at the end of April, July, October, and January, and reports taxes due the preceding quarter ending March, June, September, and December, respectively.[36] Most of the excise taxpayers using Form 720 must deposit the tax owed before filing the form with the IRS. Several excise taxes trigger a requirement to file a form in addition to Form 720 (e.g., Form 6197 [Gas Guzzler Tax], Form 2290 [Heavy Highway Vehicle Use Tax Return], and Form 6627 [Environmental Taxes]).

REVENUE

Excise taxes have had a diminishing role in federal public finance over time. Several forms of data analysis, presented in this section, illustrate this point.

One concern with per unit excise taxes is that they are often set in statute at specific levels, thus the inflation-adjusted value, or *real value*, often falls over time.[37] This trend usually continues absent legislative action to increase the statutory rates to reflect the effects of inflation.[38] The decline in the real value of excise tax receipts over time is apparent in Figure 1.

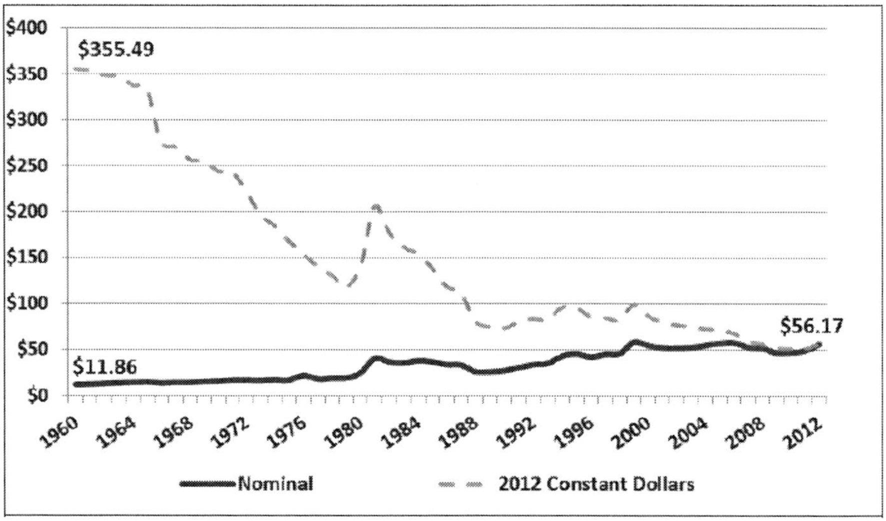

Source: CRS analysis of Internal Revenue Service, Table 6, *Databook*, 2012, at http://www.irs.gov/pub/irs-soi/ 12databk.pdf; and Office of Management and Budget, *Budget of the United States*, Historical Tables - Table 10.1, 2013, at http://www.whitehouse.gov/omb/budget/historicals.

Figure 1. Federal Excise Tax Collections, Nominal and Real Amounts, 1960 to 2012; Amounts are in billions of dollars.

Although nominal excise tax collections have increased from $11.86 billion in FY1960 to $56.17 billion in FY2012 (an increase of more than five times), real excise tax revenue has decreased by more than six times over that same period. In FY1960, excise tax collections amounted to approximately to $355.49 billion in 2012 constant dollars. The brief spike in excise tax collection during the early 1980s was largely due to the enactment of the excise tax on windfall profits in the oil industry, which was phased-out by 1993.[39] While the number, rates, and types of excise taxes in effect have changed between 1960 and 2012, these data illustrate the declining role of excise taxes in federal public finance.

Furthermore, federal excise tax receipts as a share of gross domestic product (GDP) are lower today than they were in the past. As shown in Figure 2, annual excise tax receipts averaged between 2.0% and 2.5% during the Great Depression, before hitting a peak above 3.0% of GDP during World War II. After the end of the war, federal excise tax receipts declined as a share of GDP—particularly after the reforms in the mid-1960s. After a brief spike in the early 1980s, largely due to the enactment of the oil industry windfall profits tax, excise tax revenue as a share of GDP trended back below 1.0% by the end of the 1980s. In FY2012, federal excise tax receipts were 0.5% of GDP.

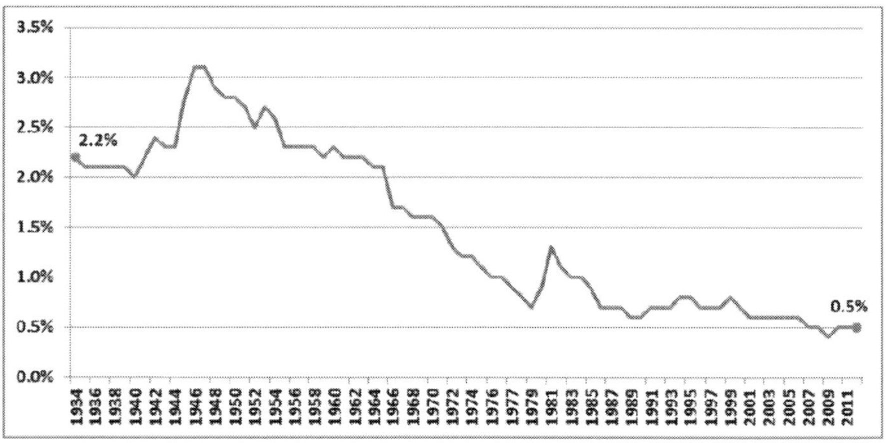

Source: Office of Management and Budget, *Budget of the United States FY2014 - Historical Tables*, Table 2.3, at http://www.whitehouse.gov/omb/budget /historicals.

Figure 2. Federal Excise Tax Receipts as a Share of Gross Domestic Product (GDP), FY1934 to FY2012.

Federal excise taxes have also declined as a share of all federal tax receipts. As shown in Figure 3, federal excise taxes comprised 45.8% of all federal tax receipts in FY1934. After the end of World War II, the share of federal tax receipts from excises began a slow decline below 15% towards a recent trend around 3.2% (in FY2012).

This decline in the share of federal tax receipts collected from excises corresponded with an increase in the role of other sources of tax receipts, notably from the individual income tax code. In 1934, individual income taxes amounted to 14.2% of all federal tax receipts and applied primarily to a narrow tax base.[40] During World War II, the individual tax code supplanted excises as being the primary source of federal revenue, as income taxes accounted for 45.0% of all tax receipts in 1944 (compared to 10.9% from excises).[41] Additionally, receipts from social insurance and retirement programs have increased over time.

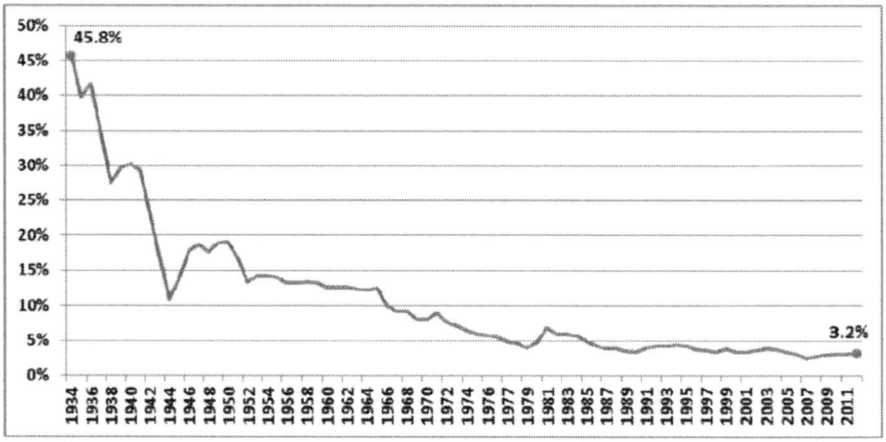

Source: Office of Management and Budget, *Budget of the United States FY2014 - Historical Tables*, Table 2.2, at http://www.whitehouse.gov/omb/budget/historicals.

Figure 3. Federal Excise Tax Receipts as a Share of All Federal Tax Receipts, FY1934 to FY2012.

Interactions between Federal and State and Local Excise Taxes

Higher federal excise tax rates tend to reduce state and local excise tax revenues derived from the same products (and *vice versa*).[42] As federal excise taxes increase the price of the targeted product, then consumer demand may decrease depending on the response of consumers.[43] This decrease in consumer demand reduces the tax base. States can increase their excise tax rates to help offset any reductions in the tax base, although higher state taxes can also drive down demand for products subject to excise taxes.

Similar to trends at the federal level, though, excise tax collections comprise a relatively small share of state and local tax revenue. As shown in Figure 4, personal property taxes were the largest source (34%) of tax revenue for state and local governments combined in 2012. Individual income taxes and general sales taxes accounted for 22% and 21% (respectively) of state and local tax collections in 2012. Excise taxes on motor fuel, tobacco, and alcohol have accounted for 5% of total tax collections.

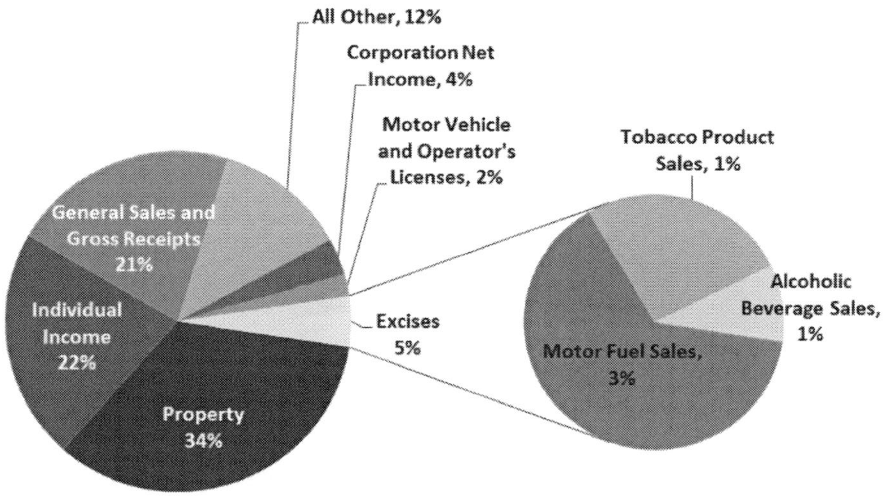

Source: CRS analysis of data from U.S. Census Bureau, Table 1 – Historical National Totals of State and Local Tax Revenue, at http://www.census.gov/govs/qtax/.

Figure 4. Sources of State and Local Tax Collections, 2012.

However, the data in Figure 4 underrepresent the amount of state tax revenue derived from tobacco sales because settlement payments from major tobacco companies to the states and territories are not included.[44] In comparison, approximately $7.3 billion in payments were made by the major tobacco companies to the states in 2011 whereas state and local tax collections from tobacco excise taxes were approximately $17.5 billion (i.e., the payments to states amounted to 41.7% of state and local excise collections).[45] Settlement payments allocated to each state and territory are largely based on tobacco consumption in that particular state or territory.

EQUITY

Economists generally measure tax equity using two measures: vertical equity and horizontal equity. Vertical equity generally implies that households with a greater ability to pay the tax (i.e., a higher income) pay a greater share of their household income in taxes than households with a lesser ability to pay the tax. A tax system is *progressive* if higher income households pay a greater share of their income in tax than lower income households, whereas the converse is true in a *regressive* tax system. Horizontal equity indicates that households with similar abilities to pay actually pay similar amounts in tax. For example, all households earning a particular amount of income would pay the same amount in taxes in a tax system with perfect horizontal equity.

Note that the excise tax rate on a particular good does not reflect its effects on equity. Even if all consumers are subject to the same tax rate of $1.00 per unit, the tax cannot be immediately deemed as "equitable" from an economic perspective. The tax's effects on equity will ultimately be a function of who bears the tax's burden.

Figure 5 shows the distribution of excise taxes paid in 2009, by average tax rates, as calculated by the Congressional Budget Office (CBO). Average tax rates represent the share of excise taxes paid as a share of pre-tax income.

With regard to vertical equity, excise taxes tend to be regressive. The lowest income quintile of taxpayers paid, on average, 1.5% of their income on excise taxes in 2009 whereas the highest quintile of taxpayers paid 0.4% of their income in excise taxes.

A luxury tax may be less regressive than other forms of excise taxes, but it could be difficult to isolate the burden of such a tax to upper-income households. First, middle-income consumers might purchase goods classified as "luxuries," such as jewelry or watches. Second, the definition of "luxury" changes over time. For example, a federal excise tax on telephone calls was first introduced in 1892 as a luxury tax to help finance the Spanish-American War. After several instances of repeal and reauthorization throughout the early 20th century, the tax remained part of the permanent tax code from 1947 until 2006.[46] Although one could make the argument in 1892 that telephone calls were "luxury" services, this was certainly not the case by the latter half of the 20th century.

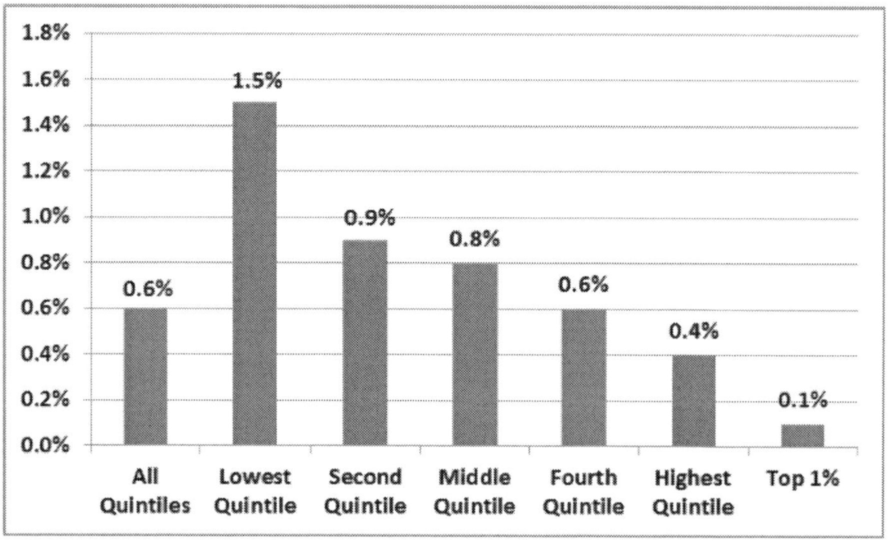

Source: Congressional Budget Office, *The Distribution of Household Income and Federal Taxes*, July 2012, pp. 27 and 33, at http://www.cbo.gov/sites/default/files/cbofiles/attachments/43373-AverageTaxRates_screen.pdf.

Notes: Average tax rates are equal to the amount of taxes paid divided by pre-tax income. The average amount of pre-tax income for each quintile in 2009 was $88,400 (all), $23,900 (lowest), $43,400 (second), $64,300 (middle), $93,800 (fourth), $223,500 (highest), and $1,219,700 (top 1%).

Figure 5. Distribution of Federal Excise Taxes, by Average Tax Rates, 2009.

With regard to horizontal equity, excise taxes have different effects on households with the same level of income. Households that consume the taxed good pay a larger share of taxes out of their current income than households that do not consume the taxed good. Excise taxes can also create horizontal inequities across consumers of a taxed product if unequal tax rates are applied to various forms of that product (e.g., beer vs. wine vs. distilled spirits).

EFFICIENCY

In short, some excise taxes are intended to affect consumer choices. As such, they reduce economic efficiency by distorting what economists characterize as economically optimal consumer behavior. This distortion could be justified, in economic terms, if there is some sort of market failure whereby the consumer's price does not capture the effect of spillover effects to society that result from consumption of the good or service. Individual consumption of certain goods and services might have negative spillover effects, or *externalities*, on society. For excise taxes intended to compensate for the social costs of certain types of consumption, economic theory suggests that the excise tax rate should be set at a level that offsets the negative costs of that consumption to society. If taxes are used this way to reflect the full cost of a particular type of economic activity to society, then excise taxes can actually lead to a more efficient allocation of resources.

General Behavioral Effects

All types of excise tax have some similar economic effects in a competitive industry.[47] In the short run, an excise tax increases the price of the taxed product (by some fraction of the tax amount), and tax burden could be shared by producers or the consumers. Next, the quantity of the product demanded is reduced. Lastly, the price received by producers for the product is also reduced (i.e., producers receive less for the product post-tax compared to pre-tax).

The exact effect depends on the responsiveness, or *elasticities*, of demand and supply for the product (or the percent change in quantity demanded or supplied, respectively, divided by the percent change in price). The increase in retail price resulting from the tax will be greater as the elasticity of supply increases and the elasticity of demand falls. The effect on quantity will be greater as both the elasticity of demand and the elasticity of supply increase.

In regard to sharing the price burden, the more inelastic the demand is, the larger the share of the tax borne by consumers. The more inelastic the supply is, the larger the share borne by producers. In the limiting cases, consumers will bear the full burden if demand is completely inelastic, whereas producers will bear the full price burden if supply is completely inelastic. Put differently, an excise tax on a product with a relatively inelastic demand will have less of an effect on consumption.[48]

Additionally, economic theory indicates that targeted excise taxes could have efficiency merits, but broadly drawn taxes that cover many product categories generally tend to lead to more distortions and reductions in economic activity than are warranted. From an efficiency perspective, the use of a broad-based tax on a wide range of activities (e.g., a general sales tax) would be preferable to a high excise tax rate on a small number of activities.[49]

Luxury Taxes

Luxury taxes are usually levied to increase progressivity in the tax system or to increase revenue, not on the basis of improving economic efficiency.

Some argue that luxury taxes in the past have dramatically reduced sales in the targeted industry. However, it is likely that demand for luxury goods is less sensitive to price changes than non-luxury goods, in part, because some luxury consumption goods are purchased by businesses rather than individuals (and could be deducted from a business's income tax returns as a business expense).

A common case study cited in the analysis of luxury taxes includes the luxury boat industry during the early 1990s. Opponents of the luxury tax argued that the yacht industry experienced drastic reductions in sales following the enactment of a 10% *ad valorem* luxury tax in the Omnibus Budget Reconciliation Act of 1990 (OBRA90). According to this logic, the imposition of the excise tax was largely to blame for the decline in sales and rise in unemployment in the industry. However, economic analysis indicates that the yacht sales were beginning to decline from their peak in 1988 (before the tax), and that sales of yachts were more sensitive to changes in personal disposable income and corporate profits after tax rather than price changes due to the tax.[50] In any case, the tax was repealed in the Omnibus Budget Reconciliation Act of 1993 (P.L. 103-66).

Sumptuary Taxes

Sumptuary tax increases are often based on market failures, relating to *externalized* costs of individual behavior associated with public health, public safety, and additional financial burdens placed on publically financed health services.[51] In short, studies measuring the respective size of the externalities for alcohol and tobacco involve very complicated, technical calculations of lifetime external costs and savings associated with alcohol and tobacco consumption that are often subject to controversy and methodological scrutiny. An advanced review of this literature is beyond the scope of this particular report. Still, studies suggest that current law per-unit tax rates on cigarettes exceed the magnitude of the estimated net externalities whereas the opposite could be true for alcohol taxes.[52]

Behavioral responses to sumptuary taxes vary by consumption good. Demand for beer is not particularly responsive to changes in price (e.g., demand is inelastic). Meta-analyses tend to find the demand for beer is more inelastic (i.e., less responsive) to changes in price than demand for either wine or distilled spirits. However, studies diverge on the question of whether demand for wine is more or less elastic than distilled spirits.[53] In comparison, CBO estimates the price elasticity of demand for cigarettes to be between (0.3) and (0.7), and that the average elasticity of the number of smokers is (0.3). In other words, a 1% increase in the price of cigarettes results in between a 0.3% and a 0.7% decrease in demand, and a 1% rise in the price of cigarettes results in roughly a 0.3% decrease in the number of smokers.[54]

Compared to a sumptuary tax on a product that is relatively elastic, a tax on a product that is relatively inelastic often results in a higher tax burden on lower-income households (due to the regressive nature of the tax) with a smaller degree of change in consumption.

Benefit-Based Taxes

If properly structured, benefit-based taxes could enhance economic efficiency by reducing the spread between private and social costs. In short, inefficiency arises because private markets tend to overproduce economic activities that lead to negative social externalities and underproduce economic activities that lead to positive externalities, absent government intervention. Theory suggests that government intervention can better incorporate social costs into the prices perceived by any one individual. However, it is often difficult to derive the "correct" tax rate that precisely accounts for the marginal social effects of an economic activity.[55]

Benefit-based taxes can affect consumer demand for public goods if the link between the tax and the use of the public good is clearly apparent. A lack of a direct link between the tax and the use of the public good could lead to declining revenues available for upkeep and maintenance of the public good. For example, one could argue that the purchase of gasoline does not necessarily lead to wear and tear on federal highways; some of this fuel could be used by drivers that commute just along local roads. Thus, many benefit-based taxes are levied on rough proxies that affect forms of consumption unrelated to the ultimate goal of the policy.

An alternative policy could include more direct forms of benefit-based taxation, but there could be a tradeoff between the targeting precision of a tax and its administrative costs. For example, although a retail tax on gasoline sales might be an imperfect proxy for highway usage, it is less complicated than administering an excise tax based on the weight and mileage of every motor vehicle using a federal highway. The costs of the latter form of tax administration might exceed the benefits.

Regulatory and Environmental Taxes

Much like benefit-based taxes, regulatory and environmental taxes are typically imposed on economic activities that generate externalities.[56] Whereas benefit-based taxes are concerned with an underproduction of some positive externality (e.g., a public good), regulatory and environmental taxes, however, are usually concerned with the overproduction of some negative externality (e.g., pollution). These negative externalities could include losses from damage to plants and animals and to their habitats, rapid deterioration to physical infrastructure, and various harmful effects on human health and mortality.

Economic theory indicates that a tax on the marginal production of these negative externalities could be used as a disincentive for harmful production processes and as a means of compensating society for the cleanup and mitigation of those externalities.

In the choice between a tax on pollution (or the regulation of some other activity with negative spillover effects on society) and a total ban on its production, economists generally prefer a tax.[57] From an economic perspective, a society's "optimum level" of pollution is usually not zero; instead, economists look to minimize total waste disposal costs. These costs could include residual waste or by-product recycling, input switching to safer materials, production modification, or other technology adoption. It can be expected that marginal pollution costs increase with increased waste disposal activities as greater investment in more advanced (and more costly) cleanup technologies and mitigation strategies is necessary. Put differently, there may be a point where the marginal cost of eliminating a particular unit of pollution may exceed the marginal benefit. The tax increases the private costs of pollution to reduce the spread between private and social costs.

To achieve optimum,economic efficiency, the excise tax rate would be set at a level such that the marginal, private cost of pollution is equal to the marginal, social benefits of production. Economic theory suggests that the tax should be imposed directly upon the activity which gives rise to the negative externality.[58]

The statutory incidence (or burden) of the tax may differ from the economic incidence, because the latter is affected by elasticities. Thus, consumers may bear some or all of the tax through higher prices.[59]

APPENDIX. REFERENCES TO CRS REPORTS ON SPECIFIC EXCISE TAXES

Affordable Care Act Taxes
*CRS CRS Report R41128, Health-Related Revenue Provisions in the Patient Protection and Affordable Care Act (ACA), by
Janemarie Mulvey
CRS Report R42971, Medical Device Excise Tax Regulations, by Andrew Nolan
Alcohol
CRS Report R41028, The Rum Excise Tax Cover-Over: Legislative History and Current Issues, by Steven Maguire
Aviation
CRS Report R42781, Federal Civil Aviation Programs: An Overview, by Bart Elias *CRS Report RS22641, Taxation of Aviation Prior to 1970, by Robert S. Kirk
Carbon Tax
CRS Report R42731, Carbon Tax: Deficit Reduction and Other Considerations, by Jonathan L. Ramseur, Jane A. Leggett, and Molly F. Sherlock CRS Report R40242, Carbon Tax and Greenhouse Gas Control: Options and Considerations for Congress, by Jonathan L. Ramseur and Larry Parker
Coal
CRS Report RS22881, Coal Excise Tax Refunds: United States v. Clintwood Elkhorn Mining Co., by Erika K. Lunder
*CRS Report RS21935, The Black Lung Excise Tax on Coal, by Salvatore Lazzari
Gasoline
CRS Report R40808, The Role of Federal Gasoline Excise Taxes in Public Policy, by Robert Pirog CRS Report R42877, Funding and Financing Highways and Public Transportation, by Robert S. Kirk and William J. Mallett *CRS Report RL30304, The Federal Excise Tax on Gasoline and the Highway Trust Fund: A Short History, by James M. Bickley
Guns and Ammunition
CRS Report R42992, Guns, Excise Taxes, and Wildlife Restoration, by M. Lynne Corn and Jane G. Gravelle
Oil Industry
CRS Report RL34689, Oil Industry Financial Performance and the Windfall Profits Tax, by Robert Pirog and Molly F. Sherlock CRS Report R43128, Oil Sands and the Oil Spill Liability Trust Fund: The Definition of "Oil" and Related Issues for Congress, by Jonathan L. Ramseur
Rubber Tires
*CRS Report RL30302, Federal Excise Tax on Tires: Where the Rubber Meets the Road, by Pamela J. Jackson
Sea Commerce, Harbor Maintenance, Boating, and Inland Waterways

CRS Report R41042, Harbor Maintenance Trust Fund Expenditures, by John Frittelli CRS Report RS22060, The Sport Fish Restoration and Boating Trust Fund, by Eugene H. Buck and M. Lynne Corn CRS Report R41430, Inland Waterways: Recent Proposals and Issues for Congress, by Charles V. Stern
Tobacco
CRS Report R40226, P.L. 111-3: The Children's Health Insurance Program Reauthorization Act of 2009, by Evelyne P. Baumrucker, Elicia J. Herz, and Jane G. Gravelle *CRS Report RS22681, The Cigarette Tax Increase to Finance SCHIP, by Jane G. Gravelle *CRS Report 97-1053, The Proposed Tobacco Settlement: Who Pays for the Health Costs of Smoking?, by Jane G. Gravelle *CRS Report 94-214, Cigarette Taxes to Fund Health Care Reform: An Economic Analysis, by Jane G. Gravelle and Dennis Zimmerman

Source: http://www.crs.gov/.

Notes: Archived reports are denoted with an [*]. Archived reports are available on the CRS webpage, but may not contain the most recent data on a particular tax. Authors of some archived reports may no longer be available at CRS.

End Notes

[1] This list is not exhaustive. For example, rationing taxes have been temporarily levied in order to reduce the consumption of critical supplies during wartime (e.g., rubber) and import duties are basically excise taxes levied on imports generally to protect domestic industries.

[2] Economists also refer to taxes applied to an activity generating negative externalities as a "Pigovian tax." This type of tax is named after economist Arthur Pigou, who developed the concept of economic externalities.

[3] Excise taxes were previously imposed on luxury vehicles, furs, yachts, etc. However, most of these provisions have either expired or have been repealed over the years.

[4] Economists generally do not view job creation as a justification for providing federal assistance to certain industries in the long run. They argue that in the long run such assistance will likely reallocate jobs within the economy, not increase them. In their view, jobs arise primarily from the size of the labor force.

[5] For a comprehensive list of federal excise taxes and their tax rates (as of 2011), see U.S. Congress, Joint Committee on Taxation, Present Law and Background Information on Federal Excise Tax Rates, committee print, 112th Cong., 1st sess., January 2011, JCS-1-11 (Washington: GPO, 2011). The JCT study classifies some provisions as "excise taxes," although these penalties are often thought of as "penalties" for certain types of behavior (e.g., the Patient Protection and Affordable Care Act's penalty for employers who do not provide "adequate" and "affordable" health care coverage to their employees).

[6] For an earlier history of federal excise taxes, see Tax Foundation, *Federal Excise Taxes*, June 1, 1956, at http://taxfoundation.org/article/federal-excise-taxes.

[7] For a more in-depth history of federal excise taxes, archived CRS reports are available from the author upon request.

[8] Steve Simon, "Alexander Hamilton and the Whiskey Tax," U.S. Department of the Treasury, http://www.ttb.gov/ public_info/special_feature.shtml.

[9] Tax Foundation, *Federal Excise Taxes*, June 1, 1956, p.9, at http://taxfoundation.org/article /federal-excise-taxes.

[10] Robert L. Einhorn, *American Taxation, American Slavery* (Chicago, IL: University of Chicago Press, 2008); and Joel S. Newman, "Slave Tax as Sin Tax: 18th and 19th Century Perspectives," *Tax Notes*, November 21, 2003.

[11] Tax Foundation, *Federal Excise Taxes*, June 1, 1956, p.9, at http://taxfoundation.org/article /federal-excise-taxes.

[12] The Revenue Act of 1861 also temporarily imposed the first income tax, which was implemented in 1862. The income tax was repealed in 1872.

[13] By comparison, trade tariffs produced from one-half to two-thirds of all revenue in the decades after the Civil War, whereas proceeds from federal land sales accounted primarily for the remainder of revenue collections. See Lance E. Davis and John Legler, "The Government in the American Economy, 1815-1902: A Quantitative Study," *The Journal of Economic History*, vol. 26, no. 4 (December 1966), pp. 514-552.

[14] During parts of this period of time, only customs duties outnumbered excise tax collections as the primary source of federal revenue.

[15] Tax Foundation, *Federal Excise Taxes*, June 1, 1956, p.11, at http://taxfoundation.org/article /federal-excise-taxes.

[16] See Table 3 in Tax Foundation, *Federal Excise Taxes*, June 1, 1956, p.14, at http://taxfoundation.org/article/federalexcise-taxes.

[17] See Revenue Act of 1940 (P.L. 76-656), Revenue Act of 1941 (P.L. 77-250), Revenue Act of 1942 (P.L. 77-753), and Revenue Act of 1943 (P.L. 78-235); and Tax Foundation, *Federal Excise Taxes*, June 1, 1956, p.17, at http://taxfoundation.org/article/federal-excise-taxes.

[18] See W.C. Bryant, "Key Republicans Toss Political Dynamite Into Laps of Leaders: Ask Excise Tax Raise," *Wall Street Journal*, October 21, 1947, p. 5.

[19] U.S. Congress, Senate Committee on Finance, *Senate Report on the Excise Tax Reduction Act of 1965*, 89th Cong., 1st sess., June 14, 1965, S. Rpt. 89-324 (Washington: GPO, 1965), p. 1. Although many of the scheduled reductions and taxes repealed by the act were delayed until the late 1960s and early 1970s. See Joseph Pechman, *Federal Tax Policy*, 3rd ed. (Washington, DC: Brookings Institution Press, 1977), p. 189.

[20] See R. Rudy Higgins-Evenson, "Financing for a Second Era of Internal Improvements," *Social Science History*, vol. 26, no. 4 (Winter 2002), pp. 623-651.

[21] For more information on financing public highways, see CRS Report R42877, *Funding and Financing Highways and Public Transportation*, by Robert S. Kirk and William J. Mallett.

[22] Congressional interest in enacting consumption taxes has been low. For example, a type of national consumption tax, a value-added-tax, has been explicitly rejected by Congress in the past. The Senate voted 85-13 on a resolution rejecting a value-added-tax (VAT) in 2010. See S.Amdt. 3724 (111th).

[23] The Congressional Budget Office (CBO) estimated in 2008 that tax on sugar sweetened beverages set at 3 cents per 12 ounces could raise $50.4 million in revenue in five years. In 2011, CBO estimated that a tax on greenhouse gas emissions could raise nearly $1.2 trillion over 10 years. See CBO, *Budget Options Volume 1: Health Care*, December 2008, p. 192, at http://www.cbo.gov/sites/default/files/cbofiles/ftpdocs/99xx/doc9925/12-18-health options.pdf; and CBO, *Reducing the Deficit: Spending and Revenue Options*, March 2011,

p. 205, at http://www.cbo.gov/sites/default/ files/cbofiles/ftpdocs/120xx/doc12085/03-10-reducingthedeficit.pdf.

[24] Sijbren Cnossen, *Excise Systems: A Global Study of the Selective Taxation of Goods and Services* (Baltimore, MD: Johns Hopkins University Press, 1977), p. 10.

[25] If taxes are used this way to reflect the full cost of a particular type of economic activity to society, then excise taxes can actually lead to a more efficient allocation of resources. This concept is discussed in more detail in the "Efficiency" section of this report.

[26] For more information on excise taxes on firearms and ammunition see CRS Report R42992, *Guns, Excise Taxes, and Wildlife Restoration*, by M. Lynne Corn and Jane G. Gravelle.

[27] The decline in the real value of per unit taxes is due, in part, to increasing real prices of the taxed commodity or activity over time.

[28] A proof gallon is a combination of alcohol content and volume. A proof gallon is the volume in gallons, multiplied by the percent alcohol, multiplied by two, and divided by 100.

[29] U.S. Department of the Treasury, Alcohol and Tobacco Tax and Trade Bureau, at http://www.ttb.gov/tax_audit/ atftaxes.shtml.

[30] CRS calculations based on Consumer Price Index for All Urban Consumers (CPI-U) for all items at http://www.bls.gov/cpi/data.htm (accessed May 23, 2013).

[31] Sijbren Cnossen, *Excise Systems: A Global Study of the Selective Taxation of Goods and Services* (Baltimore, MD: Johns Hopkins University Press, 1977), p. 15.

[32] Center for Disease Control and Prevention, "Economic Facts About U.S. Tobacco Production and Use," at http://www.cdc.gov/tobacco/data_statistics/fact_sheets/economics/econ_facts/.

[33] For more information, see CRS Report R42992, *Guns, Excise Taxes, and Wildlife Restoration*, by M. Lynne Corn and Jane G. Gravelle.

[34] Alternatively, the manufacturer could have invested the money used to pay the tax and earned a market rate of return during the period between when it paid the tax and when the good is sold along the next step of the production chain.

[35] For more information, see Internal Revenue Service, *Farmer's Tax Guide* (Publication 225), Chapter 14 – Excise Taxes, at http://www.irs.gov/publications/p225/ch14.html.

[36] CCH, Tax Research Consultant, "Excise: 100, Fundamental Concepts: Federal Excise Taxes," accessed via Intelliconnect research database on 8/12/2013.

[37] Because these calculations control for changes in the price level, economists generally compare dollar-denominated amounts over time in real terms, not nominal.

[38] For particular federal "trust funds" that are financed through excise taxes, the decline in the value of excise tax revenue can be of a concern. If the growth in spending exceeds revenue, then the trust fund could be depleted over time.

[39] Crude Oil Windfall Profit Tax Act of 1980 (P.L. 96-223).

[40] Office of Management and Budget, *Budget of the United States FY2014 - Historical Tables*, Table 2.2, at http://www.whitehouse.gov/omb/budget/historicals.

[41] The rise in income tax receipts during World War II was largely due to the enactment of the "Victory Tax" under the Revenue Act of 1942 (P.L. 77-753). The Victory Tax was a flat 5% tax (lowered to 3% in 1943) on net income over $624, with few deductions. The Individual Income Tax Act of 1944 (P.L. 78-315) repealed the Victory Tax but also raised the marginal tax rates set in statute under the individual income tax code. For more information, see Roy G. Blakey and Gladys C. Blakey, "The Federal Revenue Act of 1942," *American Political Science Review*, vol. 36, no. 6 (December 1942), pp. 1069-1082; Roy G. Blakey and Gladys C. Blakey, "Federal Revenue Legislation, 1943-1944," *American Political Science Review*, vol. 38, no. 2 (April 1944), pp. 325-330; and Paul G. Kauper,

"Significant Developments in the Law of Federal Taxation, 1941-1947: I," *Michigan Law Review*, vol. 45, no. 6 (April 1947), pp. 659-678.

[42] The actual magnitude of this effect is difficult to measure, as state and local governments have also raised excise taxes over time.

[43] These behavioral responses, or elasticities, are discussed more in the "Efficiency" section of this report.

[44] In 1998, the Attorneys General of 46 states signed the Master Settlement Agreement (MSA) with the four largest tobacco companies in the United States to settle state and territorial suits to recover billions of dollars in costs associated with treating smoking-related illnesses. Four states (Florida, Minnesota, Mississippi, and Texas) settled their tobacco cases separately from the MSA states. In short, MSA funds are allocated to the states and territories according to a formula based on estimated tobacco-related Medicaid expenditures and the number of smokers in each state and territory. The annual payments are subject to a number of adjustments, reductions, and offsets—particularly a volumeof-sales adjustment. In other words, the MSA payments are based, in part, on tobacco consumption by state or territory. For more information see National Association of Attorneys General (NAAG), "NAAG Tobacco Project," at http://www.naag.org/tobacco.php.

[45] For tobacco settlement payments to the states data, see Campaign for Tobacco-Free Kids, *Actual Tobacco Settlement Payments Received by the States, 2002-2012*, October 2012, at http://www.tobaccofreekids.org/research/factsheets/pdf/ 0365.pdf; for state and local excise tax collections data see U.S. Census Bureau, Table 1 – Historical National Totals of State and Local Tax Revenue, at http://www.census.gov/govs/qtax/.

[46] The federal tax on telephone calls was imposed temporarily from 1892 to 1902 to raise revenue to help finance the Spanish-American War. The "telephone tax" was temporarily imposed again from 1917 to 1924 to help finance U.S. efforts in World War I. The tax was reintroduced temporarily in 1932 to finance the government during the recovery from the Great Depression, and was temporarily extended until its "permanent" authorization from 1947 until 2006. For a history of the telephone tax, see Joseph J. Thorndike, "The Phone Tax: Gone but Never Forgotten," *Tax Notes*, June 1, 2006.

[47] J. Fred Giertz, "Excise Taxes," in *Encyclopedia of Taxation and Tax Policy*, ed. Joseph J. Cordes, Robert D. Ebel, and Jane G. Gravelle, 2nd ed. (Urban Institute Press, 2000). Economists also refer to competitive markets as exhibiting "pure competition," where no single participant (buyer or seller) has enough power to affect the market price of a product. In contrast, sellers in markets characterized by a single or small group of sellers with enough power to affect prices (i.e., a monopoly or oligopoly) may be able to pass more of the cost of the tax along to consumers in the form of higher prices.

[48] The magnitude of the elasticity is sometimes reported and the negative sign omitted because consumer demand is often negatively correlated with prices. The important factor is if the elasticity is less than or greater than "1." Consumer goods with an elasticity greater than "1" are considered price elastic; less than "1," price inelastic. The elasticity of demand is not necessarily constant along all price points. Economic theory indicates that consumer demand is relatively more inelastic in the short run and with larger changes in price than with smaller changes in price. In the long run, however, elasticity of demand for a product is relatively elastic as consumers adjust their behavior to changes in prices.

[49] In economic terms, this concept relates to the growth of "deadweight losses" (or "excess burdens") associated with the tax. The excess burdens of an excise tax increase roughly with the square of the tax rate (e.g., doubling the tax rate quadruples the welfare loss). See J. Fred Giertz, "Excise Taxes," in *Encyclopedia of Taxation and Tax Policy*, ed. Joseph J.

Cordes, Robert D. Ebel, and Jane G. Gravelle, 2nd ed. (Washington, DC: Urban Institute Press, 2002).

[50] This analysis is contained in CRS Report 92-149, *The Effect of the Luxury Excise Tax on the Sale of Luxury Boats*, by Dennis Zimmerman. This 1992 report is available upon request from the author of this report.

[51] With regard to correcting for negative externalities, regulation can also serve as an alternative (or complementary) policy to taxation.

[52] For the most comprehensive summary of this analysis, see archived CRS Report 94-214, *Cigarette Taxes to Fund Health Care Reform: An Economic Analysis*, by Jane G. Gravelle and Dennis Zimmerman, particularly pp. 3-6. The analysis in this CRS report is largely based on the findings of study commission by the RAND Corporation. See Willard G. Manning et al., The Costs of Poor Health Habits (Cambridge, MA: Harvard University Press, 1991). For additional support, see Congressional Budget Office, Federal Taxation of Tobacco, Alcoholic Beverages, and Motor Fuels, August 1990, p. 47, at http://www.cbo.gov/sites/default/files/cbofiles/ftpdocs/79xx/doc7951/90-cbo-039.pdf.
These studies were conducted before further increases in federal, state, and local excise taxes on cigarettes and the 1998 settlements between the major tobacco companies and the states and territories.

[53] For two examples of studies that indicate that distilled spirits are more elastic than wine, see James Fogarty, "The Demand for Beer, Wine and Spirits: A Survey of the Literature," *Journal of Economic Surveys*, vol. 24, no. 3 (2010), pp. 428-478; and Alexander C. Wagenaar, Matthew J. Salois, and Kelli A. Komro, "Effects of Beverage Alcohol Price and Tax Levels on Drinking: A Meta-Analysis of 1003 Estimates from 112 Studies," *Addiction*, vol. 104, no. 2 (2009), pp. 179-190. For an example of a study that indicates that wine is more elastic than distilled spirits, see Craig A. Gallet, "The Demand for Alcohol: A Meta-Analysis of Elasticities," *The Australian Journal of Agricultural and Resource Economics*, vol. 51, no. 2 (June 2007), pp. 121-135; and See Congressional Budget Office, *Federal Taxation of Tobacco, Alcoholic Beverages, and Motor Fuels*, August 1990, p. 72, at http://www.cbo.gov/sites/default/files/cbofiles/ ftpdocs/79xx/doc7951/90-cbo-039.pdf.

[54] Congressional Budget Office, *Raising the Excise Tax on Cigarettes: Effects on Health and the Federal Budget*, June 2012, p. vi, at http://www.cbo.gov/publication/43319.

[55] For more discussion of these issues, see Harvey S. Rosen, *Public Finance*, 7th ed. (New York, NY: McGraw-Hill, 2005), p. 93.

[56] For more background on environmental taxes, see Maureen L. Cropper and Wallace E. Oates, "Environmental Economics: A Survey," *Journal of Economic Literature*, vol. 30, no. 2 (June 1992), pp. 675-740.

[57] In theory, negative environmental and regulatory externalities could be mitigated with policies other than a tax, such as production quotas or tradable permits. Each policy option has its own advantages and disadvantages, particularly with regard to setting the price of the tax or permit or the level of the quota. For a more in-depth comparison of these policies, see A. Lans Bovenberg and Lawrence H. Goulder, *Environmental Taxation and Regulation*, National Bureau of Economic Research, NBER Working Paper 8458, September 2001, at http://www.nber.org/papers/w8458.pdf; and Don Fullerton, Andrew Leicester, and Stephen Smith, *Environmental Taxes*, National Bureau of Economic Research, NBER Working Paper 14197, July 2008, at http://www.nber.org/papers/w14197.pdf; and Frank S. Arnold, *Why Policy Makers Don't Use Environmental Taxes*, draft report prepared under cooperative agreement with the U.S. Environmental Protection Agency, January 6, 1994, at http://yosemite.epa.gov/ee/epa/eerm.nsf/vwAN/EE-0312-1.pdf/ $file/EE-0312-1.pdf.

[58] For more information, see Thomas A. Barthold, "Issues in the Design of Environmental Excise Taxes," *The Journal of Economic Perspectives*, vol. 8, no. 1 (Winter 1994), pp. 133-151.

[59] A more elastic demand (supply) indicates that consumers (producers) are more responsive to changes in price. Consumers absorb a larger share of the tax when producer supply is more elastic than consumer demand.

In: Federal Excise Taxes
Editor: Jerold M. Busch
ISBN: 978-1-62948-483-9

Chapter 2

GUNS, EXCISE TAXES, AND WILDLIFE RESTORATION*

M. Lynne Corn and Jane G. Gravelle

ABSTRACT

As a result of the recent debate over guns, gun rights, and gun-related violence, there has been a marked increase in sales of many weapons as well as ammunition. Through an excise tax on firearms and ammunition, such sales have a marked beneficial effect on funding for state wildlife programs through the Wildlife Restoration Program (also known as Pittman-Robertson or P-R). This report examines these taxes, their allocation, and their use. It also examines the effects of sequestration of this account, pursuant to the Budget Control Act of 2011 (BCA; P.L. 112-25).

THE EXCISE TAXES

The Pittman-Robertson Wildlife Restoration Act of 1937 (16 U.S.C. 669-669k; P-R) uses the proceeds from a federal excise tax to fund grants to states and territories for projects to benefit wildlife resources and to conduct

* This is an edited, reformatted and augmented version of Congressional Research Service, Publication No. R42992, dated March 18, 2013.

programs for hunter education. The excise tax predates the act, having begun in 1919. The excise tax is set at 10% of the wholesale price for pistols and revolvers, and 11% for other firearms as well as shells or cartridges,[1] and is collected by the manufacturer. An 11% tax on archery equipment is also deposited into the fund. The tax is applied whether the equipment is likely to be used for hunting or not. Total collections from these taxes were $388.2 million in FY2011 and $555.3 million in FY2012. Most of the tax is collected from firearms and ammunition. Of the tax on firearms and ammunition, approximately one-third is due to each source: 31% for pistols and revolvers, 37% for other firearms, and 31% for ammunition.[2] These amounts become available for expenditure in the year following their collection.[3] (See Figure 1.)

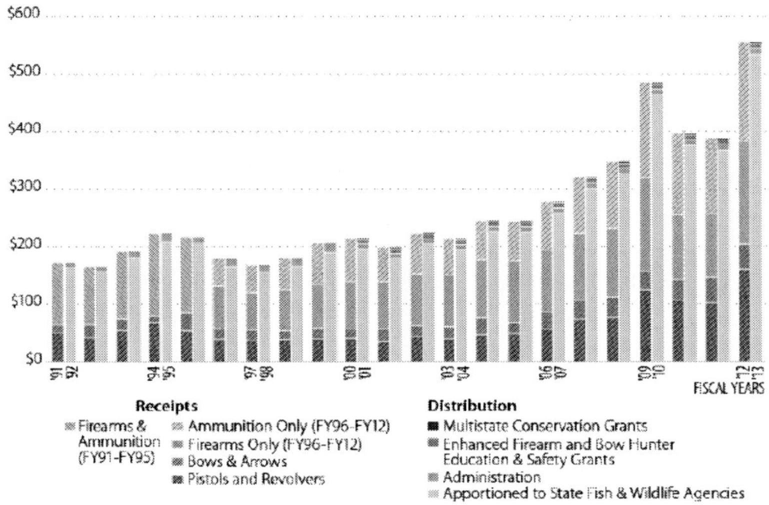

Source: Steve Barton, acting deputy assistant director, and chief, Division of Administration and Information Management, Wildlife and Sport Fish Restoration Program, FWS. Personal email to Lynne Corn, February 13, 2013. FWS tabular data converted to bar graph by CRS. FY2013 expenditures shown here do not reflect the effects of sequestration. See text.

Notes: Funds become available in the year following collection, so each year of collection is paired with the following year's distribution. Up through FY1995, collections for the sale of firearms and ammunition were lumped together, and so are shown together above. In FY1996, collections from ammunition and firearms began to be tabulated separately, as reflected in the chart.

Figure 1. Pittman-Robertson Receipts and Distributions, FY1991-FY2013; ($ in millions).

The P-R tax has some of the same exemptions and tax-free sales as those that typically apply to excise taxes: sales are tax-free to the Department of Defense and the Coast Guard, for use in vessels and aircraft, to state and local governments, to nonprofits, and for export. Producers of less than 50 guns a year are exempt. There is also a personal use exemption for manufacturers, importers, or producers who incidentally produce for their own use. There are no data on the revenue loss due to exemptions, although the personal exemption would be expected to be small.

The tax is currently administered by the Alcohol and Tobacco Tax and Trade Bureau (TTB) in the Department of the Treasury. It was formerly administered by the Bureau of Alcohol, Tobacco and Firearms (ATF) from 1991 until its transfer and prior to that by the Internal Revenue Service.[4]

Because the taxes are allocated to wildlife restoration and hunter education, the tax appears to be motivated as a use tax (to support the activities of those taxed), much like gasoline taxes that pay for roads, and not as a "sin" tax, such as those on alcohol and tobacco that go into the general fund.

THE PITTMAN-ROBERTSON FUND: ALLOCATION AND USE

The revenues from these excise taxes go into a special account called the Wildlife Restoration Fund or P-R Fund, administered by the Fish and Wildlife Service (FWS) in the Department of the Interior.[5] Amounts are available for expenditure in the year following their collection. Appropriations from the fund are mandatory spending to the extent of receipts; FWS may deduct administrative expenses from the receipts. There is currently a limit of 3% specified in law for administrative expenses, and the law limits the types of administrative expenses that may be charged to the fund.[6] Any interest that may accrue on moneys in the fund before they are spent is allocated to the North American Wetlands Conservation Fund (NAWCF), rather than being retained in the P-R Fund.

Distribution of moneys in the fund is by formula. First, $8 million is set aside for Enhanced Hunter Education, which provides for the construction or maintenance of public target ranges, with limits on the maximum and minimum amounts a state or territory may receive. States and territories must match at least 25% of the cost of a project, although the match requirement may be waived for some territories.[7] In some cases, states provide more than the minimum match. Second, $3 million is set aside to supplement projects that involve cooperation between or among states. Third, one-half of the excise tax on pistols, revolvers, bows, and arrows (but not firearms) is to be set aside for Basic Hunter Education. In FY2013, this amount is estimated at $71.5 million.[8] This portion is also allocated according to a formula among the states and territories, with the same minimum matching requirements.

The remaining amount forms the bulk of the program. A small percent of the remainder is allocated first to the territories of American Samoa, Guam, Puerto Rico, Virgin Islands, and Northern Mariana Islands. Then the remainder of the fund is divided in half, with one half allocated in proportion to the area of the state, and the other half in proportion to the number of paid hunting licenses in the state relative to paid hunting licenses in the entire country.[9] Together, the Basic Hunter Education program and the Wildlife Restoration grants were $388.2 million in FY2012, and are estimated at $533.8 million in FY2013, again not accounting for the effect of sequestration. (See Figure 1.) A preliminary apportionment is made to the states and territories each October based on early data concerning receipts; a final apportionment of the remainder is made in the following February. With reports of surges in gun sales due to current controversies over guns rights and gun-related violence,[10] substantially more funds seem likely to be available in FY2014.

History of Increased Sales

Among the sportsmen's community and among state wildlife agencies, the P-R program is not considered controversial, because the link between these users who pay the tax and the beneficiaries is clear. Even those who purchase taxable items that are never used in hunting may benefit from the portion of the P-R program devoted to shooting ranges and the training offered under the hunter education program. Moreover, while game species and their habitats are the primary or direct beneficiaries of the program, non-game species, such as native plants, non-game birds, and other species, may benefit incidentally through conservation of the habitats they share with hunted species. The result is additional support from groups outside the traditional hunting community. While some items subject to the tax are rarely used in hunting, their inclusion in the program is not known to be an issue. As a result of these and other factors, the P-R program has been relatively noncontroversial through much of its 75-year history. The increase in sales of guns and related items in the months before the passage of the Violent Crime Control and Law Enforcement

Act of 1994 (P.L. 103-322), in the months before the elections of 2008 and 2012, and during the current debate over gun rights and gun violence have all benefitted wildlife conservation via the P-R program. However, as the amounts available under P-R grants increase, and as state budgets are constrained, some states may be unable to make full use of available funds because they cannot supply the minimum local match.

SEQUESTRATION OF PITTMAN-ROBERTSON FUND

The Office of Management and Budget, based on the Budget Control Act of 2011 (BCA, P.L. 112-25), determined that P-R (as a non-exempt, nondefense mandatory program) is subject to sequestration. The *OMB Report to the Congress on the Joint Committee Sequestration for Fiscal Year 2013* states:

> The Balanced Budget and Emergency Deficit Control Act, as amended (BBEDCA), 2 U.S.C. § 901a, requires the Office of Management and Budget (OMB) to calculate, and the President to order on March 1, 2013, reductions in budgetary resources triggered by the failure of the Joint Select Committee on Deficit Reduction to propose, and the Congress to enact, legislation to reduce the deficit by $1.2 trillion (Joint Committee sequestration). This report provides OMB's calculations of the percentage and dollar amount of the reduction for each non-exempt budget account and an explanation of the calculations.
>
> OMB calculates that the Joint Committee sequestration requires a [reduction of] ... 5.1 percent to other non-exempt nondefense mandatory programs.[11]

In the appendix to the report, OMB estimates that the P-R budget authority for FY2013 is $413 million.[12] With a 5.1% reduction, $21 million would be sequestered under current law (OMB report, p. 35). It is unclear what happens to the sequestered amount—it may become available in subsequent years.[13]

The ultimate reduction to P-R could differ from what is listed in the report. Some in Congress have objected to the BCA reductions. Consequently, the sequestration rules specified in P.L. 112- 25 might be changed in a new law, or an agreement might be reached on alternative changes to the federal budget that would meet required targets. The effects of such actions on P-R could differ from the sequestered amounts projected in the OMB Report.

Those who receive the benefits of the P-R program (the state wildlife agencies and, through them, hunters and other wildlife enthusiasts) strongly overlap the group of people who pay for it (purchasers of guns, ammunition, and archery equipment). The payers will continue to pay the current excise taxes on the specified items, but the expenditures for the program will be reduced under sequestration, so that 94.9% of the taxes collected will be available to the program and 5.1% are sequestered. State wildlife agencies and hunting organizations have objected to this outcome,[14] and the controversy may become part of the larger debate over sequestration.

End Notes

[1] Certain weapons and manufacturers are subject to separate taxes based on the National Firearms Act and subsequent legislation. These are weapons that, in private hands, are older collectibles and are rare. The regulation of these weapons is by the Bureau of Alcohol, Tobacco, Firearms, and Explosives (ATF). The resulting amounts appear inconsequential.

[2] Data on the distribution of taxes between pistols and revolvers, other firearms, and ammunition provided by Thomas K. Hogue of the Alcohol and Tobacco Tax and Trade Bureau (TTB); data are for FY2012. The total collection was $483.1 million. The information was provided with the following notation: "These figures represent tax liabilities reported on returns filed as of January 28, 2013 (the date the attached report was run) and are only accurate as of that date. These figures do not represent taxes collected. Late filed or amended tax returns will increase or decrease the tax liability for these periods. Future TTB statistical releases will include the updated liabilities and therefore will not agree with the figures provided in this email."

[3] Steve Barton, Acting Deputy Assistant Director, and Chief, Division of Administration and Information Management, Wildlife and Sport Fish Restoration Program, FWS. Personal email to Lynne Corn, February 13, 2013. These and other figures on collections and expenditures in this report are derived from this source unless otherwise specified.

[4] Under the Homeland Security Act (P.L. 107-296), Congress established TTB at the Department of the Treasury. The TTB generally consists of those administrative units charged with regulating alcohol and tobacco products that were previously housed in Treasury's Bureau of Alcohol, Tobacco and Firearms (ATF). In the act, Congress also changed the title of ATF to include explosives—the Bureau of Alcohol, Tobacco, Firearms and Explosives (still ATF)—and transferred it to the Department of Justice. While ATF remains responsible for most all aspects of regulating and enforcing firearms and explosives laws, as well as enforcing some aspects of alcohol and tobacco laws, Congress charged TTB with administering the P-R firearms, ammunition, and archery equipment excise tax provisions.

[5] For further information about the fund, see the FWS website at http://wsfrprograms.fws.gov /Subpages/ GrantPrograms/WR/WR_Funding.htm.

[6] 16 U.S.C. 669h.

[7] The waiver provision for territories is found in 48 U.S.C. 1469a(d). U.S. territories eligible for the waiver American Samoa, Guam, Commonwealth of the Northern Mariana Islands, and

Virgin Islands. Puerto Rico is not eligible for the waiver; the District of Columbia is not eligible for the P-R program.

[8] FWS *Budget Justification and Performance Information for Fiscal Year 2013*, pp. WR-9 –WR-10. Estimate does not include the effect of sequestration.

[9] This formula does not distinguish between in-state and out-of-state hunters. A hunting license purchased by a nonresident would count the same under this formula as one purchased by a resident.

[10] Michael Cooper, "Sales of Guns Soar in U.S. as Nation Weighs Tougher Limits," *New York Times*, January 11, 2013, available at http://www.nytimes.com/2013/01/12/us/as-us-weighs-new-rules-sales-of-guns-and-ammunitionsurge.html?_r=0.

[11] *OMB Report to the Congress on the Joint Committee Sequestration for Fiscal Year 2013*, p. 1, available at http://www.whitehouse.gov/sites/default/files/omb/assets/legislative_reports /fy13ombjcsequestrationreport.pdf.

[12] The OMB estimate of P-R budget authority for FY2013 appears to be conservative, and differs from the $555.3 million that FWS estimated in collections for FY2012. The reason for this difference is unclear.

[13] P-R is called, technically, a *special account*. Under the BCA Section 256(k)(6) of the Balanced Budget and Emergency Deficit Control Act of 1985, as amended (2 U.S.C. 906(k)(6)): "(6) Budgetary resources sequestered in revolving, trust, and special fund accounts and offsetting collections sequestered in appropriation accounts shall not be available for obligation during the fiscal year in which the sequestration occurs, but shall be available in subsequent years to the extent otherwise provided in law."

[14] For example, see National Rifle Association, "OMB Threatens Pittman-Robertson Funds," at http://www.nrahuntersrights.org/Article.aspx?id=7299. Viewed on March 12, 2013.

In: Federal Excise Taxes
Editor: Jerold M. Busch

ISBN: 978-1-62948-483-9

Chapter 3

Medical Device Excise Tax Regulations*

Andrew Nolan

Summary

On December 7, 2012, the Department of the Treasury and the Internal Revenue Service issued final regulations explaining the scope of the medical device excise tax created by the Health Care and Education Reconciliation Act of 2010 (HCERA), which modified the Patient Protection and Affordable Care Act of 2010. The new regulations were issued less than a month before the 2.3% excise tax took effect on January 1, 2013. This report provides a brief overview of the recently enacted Treasury regulations and the legal implications of the regulations.

The Treasury regulations on the medical device excise tax explain both who is subject to the excise tax and the scope of the statutory exemptions provided for the tax. Specifically, the regulations incorporate by reference the general definitions for a "manufacturer, producer, or importer" outlined in the Internal Revenue Code, meaning that the excise tax will be directly paid by manufacturers, as opposed to consumers or others that use a given medical device.

Furthermore, the regulations attempt to clarify the limits to the medical device excise tax. Beyond the statutory exemptions created for eyeglasses, contact lenses, and hearing aids, the law created a "retail

* This is an edited, reformatted and augmented version of Congressional Research Service, Publication No. R42971, dated February 26, 2013.

exemption" to the excise tax, excluding from the tax medical devices that are "generally purchased by the general public at retail for individual use." The Treasury regulations attempt to simultaneously provide certainty to potential taxpayers as to which devices are subject to the retail exemption, while allowing the government the flexibility to properly apply the retail exemption to the variety of devices that could be exposed to the excise tax. The regulations provide a flexible two-prong test to determine whether a device should fall within the retail exemption, applying the exemption when the device is (1) regularly available for purchase by non-professional consumers and (2) not primarily intended for use by medical professionals. The regulations provide several factors to consider when applying the two-prong test. To provide some certainty to the scope of the retail exemption, the regulations also included several "safe harbor" provisions, explicitly acknowledging that certain devices, such as "over-the-counter" devices, fall within the retail exemption.

The new Treasury regulations on the medical device excise tax, while providing some certainty with respect to what devices will be exempt from the tax, generally favor a more flexible approach to defining the scope of the central exemption to the tax. As a consequence, uncertainty remains as to which medical devices will be subject to the tax. Indeed, Treasury, in releasing the medical device excise tax regulations, notes that further clarification on various issues implicated by the tax is still needed. As such, the regulations constitute only the first step in defining the limits of the medical device excise tax.

INTRODUCTION

As part of recent health care reform efforts, Congress, in the Affordable Care Act,[1] imposed a 2.3% excise tax on the sale of certain medical devices by device manufacturers, producers, or importers.[2] The excise tax is effective on sales of devices made after December 31, 2012.[3] The implementation of the medical device tax has prompted some Members of Congress to seek a delay of the enforcement of the tax out of a concern that the "uncertainty and confusion" regarding compliance with the medical device excise tax will harm the medical technology industry.[4] Others in Congress have sought an outright repeal of the tax.[5] While December 31, 2012, passed without Congress changing or repealing the medical device excise tax, congressional interest remains.[6] On December 7, 2012, the Department of the Treasury (Treasury) issued its final regulations that provide guidance on both who must pay the excise tax and the scope of products encompassed by the excise tax.[7] This report provides a brief overview of the regulations and discusses the extent to which the rules have clarified the excise tax imposed on the sale of medical devices.[8]

On Whom Is the Medical Device Excise Tax Imposed?

Pursuant to §4191(a) of the Internal Revenue Code (IRC), a "manufacturer, producer, or importer" making the sale of a taxable medical device is liable for a tax of 2.3% of the price[9] for which the device was sold.[10] Treasury, in the newly released regulations on the medical device excise tax, states that the "existing chapter 32 rules," including the definitions for "manufacturer," "producer," and "importer," apply with respect to the medical device excise tax.[11] In turn, the general chapter 32 rules define the term "manufacturer" as "any person who produces a taxable article ... by processing, manipulating, or changing the form of an article or by combining or assembling two or more articles."[12] Moreover, the general definition for a manufacturer necessarily includes the terms "producer" and "importer."[13] While courts have interpreted the term "manufacturer" within the general chapter 32 rules to encompass a range of activities where a person physically changes a taxable article, [14] the medical device excise tax, by definition, is not directly levied upon a consumer of a medical device.

What Is a "Taxable Medical Device"?

The medical device excise tax created by the ACA is imposed on the sale of "taxable medical device[s]."[15] The statute defines that term by incorporating the definition of "medical device" from the Federal Food, Drug and Cosmetic Act (FFDCA), as that term pertains to a device "intended for humans."[16] Courts have recognized that Congress defined the term "medical device" in the FFDCA "very broadly,"[17] as the FDA regulates a range of devices from tongue depressors[18] to artificial hearts.[19] As such, the Health Care and Education Reconciliation Act of 2010 (HCERA) casts a wide net with the term "taxable medical device."[20] In line with the broad scope of the term "taxable medical device," the December 7, 2012, Treasury Regulations explain that a "taxable medical device" is a device that has been registered with the Food and Drug Administration pursuant to Section 510(j) of the FFDCA[21] and 21

C.F.R. Part 807.[22] Importantly, Treasury resisted efforts by commenters to narrow the scope of the general term "taxable medical device," by limiting, for example, the term to devices that could exclusively be used by humans or could only be used for a medical purpose, preferring instead to maintain a broad reading of what devices are subject to the excise tax.[23] As a result, devices like infusion pumps, which can be used on both humans and animals, [24] and latex gloves,[25] which can be used for both medical and non-medical purposes, fall within the broad definition of a "taxable medical device."

MEDICAL DEVICES EXEMPTED FROM THE EXCISE TAX

In an effort to limit the ambit of the excise tax imposed on medical device manufacturers, Congress explicitly excluded three types of devices from the term "taxable medical device" in IRC §4191(a).[26] Specifically, Congress exempted eyeglasses, contact lenses, and hearing aids from the excise tax.[27] Moreover, the statute empowers the Secretary of the Treasury under the "retail exemption" to exempt "any other medical device" which is determined to be of a "type which is generally purchased by the general public at retail for individual use" from the 2.3% excise tax.[28]

The Retail Exemption

The regulations issued by Treasury on December 7, 2012, provide a broad framework as to which medical devices fall within the "retail exemption" to the excise tax under IRC §4191(b)(2)(d). Specifically, the new Treasury regulations provide a two-prong test to resolve whether a device should fall within the residual exception to the excise tax.[29] First, the device in question should be "regularly available for purchase and use by individual consumers who are not medical professionals." Second, the device's design should "demonstrate[] that it is not primarily intended for use" in a medical institution, office, or by a medical professional.[30] Neither prong is dispositive to the determination, as the regulations caution that an analysis of whether a device fits within the retail exemption is dependent on "all" "relevant facts and circumstances."[31]

To guide the analysis of whether a particular device meets the relevant requirements for the retail exemption, the new Treasury regulations provide a host of factors to examine.[32] Factors implicating the question of whether a device is regularly available for purchase by individual consumers include (1) the ability of end consumers to purchase the device in person through a drug store or other retailer that primarily sells a particular device; (2) the need of a consumer to seek help from a medical professional to use the device safely and effectively; and (3) whether the device has been classified by the Food and Drug Administration as a "physical medicine device" for human use.[33] To illustrate, with respect to adhesive bandages,[34] an application of the multi-factor test would conclude that the device is regularly available for purchase by individual consumers. Specifically, while adhesive bandages are not a "physical medicine device," the product can be readily purchased at various retail stores and can be properly used without formal training from a medical professional.[35]

Treasury also issued a list of factors to aid the determination of whether a device is designed primarily for use in a medical institution or office or by a medical professional.[36] Relevant factors include (1) whether the device must be implanted, inserted, operated, or administered by a medical professional; (2) the cost of obtaining and using the device; (3) how the device has been classified by the FDA;[37] and (4) whether the device is one for which payment is available "exclusively on a rental basis" and is an item requiring "frequent and substantial servicing" as those terms are defined under Medicare Part B payment rules.[38] Returning to the example of adhesive bandages, the multi-factor test counsels that the product is not primarily intended for use in a medical institution, office, or by a medical professional. Specifically, using adhesive bandages does not require the aid of a medical professional, and bandages are inexpensive to obtain and use.[39] Moreover, adhesive bandages are not classified as a complex medical device or a device needing frequent and substantial servicing.[40] Coupled with the earlier conclusion that adhesive bandages are regularly available for purchase by individual consumers, the totality of the circumstances indicates that "adhesive bandages are devices that are of a type that" should fall within the retail exemption to the medical device excise tax.[41]

Notably, Treasury explained in issuing the medical device excise tax regulations that two potential factors—the packaging or labeling of a medical device and the nature of documents submitted to the FDA in obtaining approval of a device—are irrelevant in assessing whether a device should fall within the retail exemption to the excise tax.[42] As a consequence, a medical device manufacturer cannot hope to escape the excise tax, for example, by labeling that its product is "intended for retail use only."

The Retail Exemption's Safe Harbor Provisions

In contrast to the malleable multi-factor test that outlines the limits to the retail exemption, the December 7, 2012, Treasury regulations also include a list of "safe harbor" devices that necessarily fall within the retail exemption.[43] The purpose of the safe harbor provisions is to "provide greater certainty" with respect to which devices are subject to the retail exemption.[44] The safe harbor includes medical devices, like pregnancy test kits, that are described as "over-the-counter" (OTC) devices in the FDA's online database for *in vitro* diagnostic tests, the FDA's classification regulations, or the FDA's device registration and listing database.[45] In addition, the safe harbor includes certain devices that qualify as "durable medical equipment, prosthetics, orthotics, and supplies" for which payment is available on a purchase basis under Medicare part B payment rules,[46] such as therapeutic shoes.[47]

Examples of How the Retail Exemption Is Applied

The Treasury regulations conclude by providing 15 different examples of how the retail exemption to the medical device excise tax would be applied in practice.[48] The examples range from the aforementioned "adhesive bandages"[49] to "blood glucose monitors"[50] to "magnetic resonance systems."[51] Examples of devices that Treasury concludes "based on the totality of the facts and circumstances" fall within the retail exemption include "absorbent tipped applicators,"[52] "adhesive bandages,"[53] "snake bite suction kits,"[54] "denture adhesives,"[55] "mechanical and powered wheelchairs,"[56] "portable oxygen concentrators,"[57] and "therapeutic AC powered adjustable home use beds."[58] Treasury also concludes that "pregnancy test kits,"[59] "blood glucose monitors, test strips, and lancets,"[60] "prosthetic legs and certain prosthetic leg components,"[61] and "urinary ileostomy bags"[62] fall within the regulations' safe harbor provisions. In contrast, Treasury, in its examples, finds that the following devices, based on the totality of the circumstances, are not exempt from the medical device excise tax: "mobile x-ray systems,"[63] "nonabsorbable silk sutures,"[64] "nuclear magnetic resonance imaging systems,"[65] and "powered floatation therapy beds."[66]

ISSUES THAT REMAIN FOR THE MEDICAL DEVICE TAX

Whether the new Treasury regulations provide the needed clarity to alleviate the "uncertainty and confusion" that some Members of Congress have feared that the new tax would engender within the medical technology industry remains to be seen.[67] To be sure, the medical device tax regulations, with their safe harbor provisions, clarify that generally devices recognized as over-the-counter devices will not be the subject of the tax, providing an easy to understand exemption to manufacturers, importers, and producers of such products.[68] However, the safe harbor provisions are narrow, and the regulations open-ended two-part test defining the limits of the retail exemption, while providing flexibility as to the scope of the exemption, naturally creates ambiguity with respect to which products are exposed to the excise tax, save those specifically exempted under the regulations. Moreover, the limits of the retail exemption, which are based, in part, on regulations that were not crafted with the retail exemption in mind, could prove to be either over or under inclusive of Congress's original intent in enacting the medical device excise tax.[69] Treasury, in the release of the final regulations, identified several issues raised by the medical device tax regulations that warranted the agency issuing separate clarifying guidance, including the treatment, for purposes of the medical device excise tax, of licensing software [70] and "kits."[71] Given the wide variety of items that are categorized as medical devices,[72] some may see a need for further clarification with respect to other medical devices, including potentially expanding the safe harbor provisions. As a result, the December 7, 2012, regulations could be only the first step in clarifying the application of a tax that the Treasury Department acknowledges "may present certain implementation challenges."[73]

End Notes

[1] The medical device excise tax was included in an amended version of the Affordable Care Act. *See* Health Care and Education Reconciliation Act of 2010, P.L. 111-152, Title I, Subtitle E, §1405(a)(1), 124 Stat. 1029, (2010) (amending the Patient Protection and Affordable Care Act of 2010, P.L. 111-148).

[2] *See* I.R.C. §4191(a). The medical device excise tax is only one of several provisions created under the HCERA or Patient Protection and Affordable Care Act to raise revenues to pay for expanded health insurance coverage. *See* CRS Report R41128, *Health-Related Revenue Provisions in the Patient Protection and Affordable Care Act (ACA)*, by Janemarie Mulvey.

[3] *See supra* footnote 1, §1405(c). For medical devices financed through an installment sale or a long-term lease, the regulations do not provide any relief for payments made for a device after December 31, 2012, unless that agreement was entered into prior to March 30, 2010, the date the ACA was enacted. *See* Treas. Reg. §48.4191-1(f) (citing Treas. Reg. §48.4216(c)-1(e)).

[4] *See* Letter to the Honorable Harry Reid from 18 Current and Future Members of the Senate, (December 4, 2012) http://www.franken.senate.gov/?p=hot_topic&id=2248.

[5] A bill repealing the medical device excise tax passed the House of Representatives in the 112th Congress. *See* Health Care Cost Reduction Act of 2012, H.R. 436 (2012).

[6] *See, e.g.,* Melissa Attias and Emily Ethridge, *Medicare Board, Device Tax Lead House GOP Target List*, Roll Call, January 22, 2013, http://www.cq.com/doc/news-4208077?wr=eFF6UlQqRXM3azJhbDBGWEpQWjBIUQ.

[7] *See* "Taxable Medical Devices," 77 Fed. Reg. 72,924 (December 7, 2012).

[8] This report does not discuss the general Treasury regulations for manufacturer excise taxes unless those regulations uniquely impact the medical device excise tax.

[9] For explanation of the definition of the "price" of an article taxed under Chapter 32 of the Internal Revenue Code, *see* I.R.C. §4216(a).

[10] *See* I.R.C. §4191(a).

[11] *See* 77 Fed. Reg. at 72930. Notably, the general exemptions for excise taxes provided to manufacturers who sell an article to a state or local government or to a nonprofit educational organization do not apply to the medical device excise tax. *See* I.R.C. §4221(a).

[12] *See* Treas. Reg. §48.0-2(4)(i). The general definitions for a manufacturer, producer, and importer are incorporated by reference into the regulations clarifying the medical device excise tax. *See* Treas. Reg. §48.4191-1(c). The Internal Revenue Code does not subject a manufacturer to an excise tax if the sale of the article is for use by the purchaser for further manufacturing. *See* I.R.C. §4221(a)(1).

[13] *Id.* Treasury regulations also explain that the term "importer," while typically entailing the person who brings an "article into the United States from a source outside the United States," can also include the beneficial owner of an item if, for example, a customs broker is engaged by an entity to bring a particular item into the country. *Id.* In contrast, the Internal Revenue Code exempts a manufacturer from being subject to an excise tax when the sale of the article is for export. *See* I.R.C. §4221(a)(2).

[14] *See Ruan Financial Corp. v. United States*, 765 F. Supp. 987-88 (S.D. Iowa 1990), *aff'd* 976 F.2d 452 (8th Cir. 1992).

[15] I.R.C. §4191(a).

[16] *Id.* at (b)(1) (citing 21 U.S.C. §321(h)).

[17] *See Committee of Dental Amalgam Mfrs. & Distribs. v. Stratton*, 92 F.3d 807, 810 (9th Cir. 1996); *see also United States v. McGuff,* 781 F. Supp. 654, 655 (C.D. Cal. 1991).

[18] 21 C.F.R. §880.6230.

[19] 21 C.F.R. Part 870, subpart D.

[20] Specifically, the Food, Drug, and Cosmetics Act defines a medical device as an "instrument, apparatus, implement, machine, contrivance, implant, in vitro reagent, or other similar or related article including any component, parts or accessory which is" either (1) "recognized in the official National Formulary, or the United States Pharmacopeia, or any supplement to them," (2) "intended for use in the diagnosis of disease or other conditions, or in the cure, mitigation, treatment, or prevention of disease, or other animals," or (3) "intended to affect the structure or any function of the body of man or other animals, and which does not achieve its primary intended purposes through chemical action within or on the body of man

or other animals and which is not dependent upon being metabolized for the achievement of its primary intended purposes." *See* 21 U.S.C. §321(h).

[21] 21 U.S.C. §360(j).

[22] For a general explanation of the medical device regulatory framework, *see* CRS Report R42130, *FDA Regulation of Medical Devices*, by Judith A. Johnson. Devices used exclusively in veterinary medicine are not listed under Section 510(j) of the FFDCA and 21 CFR Part 807, and, therefore, Treasury's regulations are exclusive to devices that are intended, at least in part, for use on humans.

[23] 77 Fed. Reg. at 72,925-26. However, medical kits created by a hospital or medical institution are exempt from the excise tax, as the creations of such kits are necessarily excluded from the FDA's registration and listing requirements. *See* 21 C.F.R. §807.65(f).

[24] *See* Food and Drug Administration, *How FDA Regulates Veterinary Devices*, (January 20, 2012), http://www.fda.gov/AnimalVeterinary/ResourcesforYou/ucm047117.htm.

[25] 21 C.F.R. §880.6250.

[26] I.R.C. §4191(b)(2).

[27] *Id.* §4191(b)(2)(A)-(C).

[28] *Id.* §4191(b)(2)(D); *see also* Joint Committee on Taxation, *General Explanation of Tax Legislation Enacted in the 111th Congress*, committee print, prepared by Staff of the Joint Committee on Taxation, 111th Cong., March 2011, JCS-2-11, p. 366 ("The Secretary may determine that a specific medical device is exempt under the provision if the device is generally sold at retail establishments (including over the internet) to individuals for their personal use.")

[29] Treas. Reg. §48.4191-2(b)(2).

[30] *Id.*

[31] *Id.*

[32] *Id.*

[33] For more detail on the factors implicating whether a device can be considered regularly available for purchase and use by individual consumers, *see* Treas. Reg. §48.4191-2(b)(2)(i)(A)-(C). With respect to devices classified by the FDA as a "physical medicine device," such devices are listed under subpart D of 21 CFR part 890, and include devices such as canes, *see* 21 C.F.R. §890.3075, crutches, *id.* §890.3150, and wheelchairs, *id.* §§890.3850 - 890.3860.

[34] *See* Treas. Reg. §48.4191-2(b)(2)(iv)(Example 2).

[35] *Id.*

[36] *See* Treas. Reg. §48.4191-2(b)(2)(ii)(A)-(E).

[37] The regulations specifically cite as a factor a devices' classification as a Class III device, the medical devices subject to the most intensive pre-market screening by the FDA, *see* CRS Report R42130, *FDA Regulation of Medical Devices*, by Judith A. Johnson, to be relevant in determining whether a device should be subject to the retail exemption. *See* Treas. Reg. §48.4191-2(b)(2)(ii)(C). In addition, the new Treasury regulations explain that the FDA's classification of a device under one of fifteen various categories of medical devices in the Code of Federal Regulations is an additional factor to examine when determining whether to apply the retail exemption. *Id.* §48.4191-2(b)(2)(ii)(D).

[38] *See* Treas. Reg. §48.4191-2(b)(2)(ii)(D) (citing 42 C.F.R. part 210).

[39] *See* Treas. Reg. §48.4191-2(b)(2)(iv)(Example 2).

[40] *Id.*

[41] *Id.*

[42] 77 Fed. Reg. at 72,929.

[43] *See* Treas. Reg. §48.4191-2(b)(iii).
[44] *Id.* at 72927.
[45] *See* Treas. Reg. §48.4191-2(b)(2)(iii)(A)-(C).
[46] *Id.* §48.4191-2(b)(2)(iii)(D).
[47] *Id.* §48.4191-2(b)(2)(iii)(D)(4).
[48] *Id.* §48.4191-2(b)(2)(iv).
[49] *Id.* (Example 2).
[50] *Id.* (Example 7).
[51] *Id.* (Example 13).
[52] *Id.* (Example 1).
[53] *Id.* (Example 2).
[54] *Id.* (Example 3).
[55] *Id.* (Example 4).
[56] *Id.* (Example 9).
[57] *Id.* (Example 10).
[58] *Id.* (Example 14).
[59] *Id.* (Example 6).
[60] *Id.* (Example 7).
[61] *Id.* (Example 8).
[62] *Id.* (Example 11).
[63] *Id.* (Example 5).
[64] *Id.* (Example 12).
[65] *Id.* (Example 13).
[66] *Id.* (Example 15).
[67] *See supra* footnote 4.
[68] *See* Treas. Reg. §48.4191-2(b)(2)(iii)(A)-(C).
[69] Several of the factors used to determine the scope of the retail exemption are FDA regulations relating to safety controls on the release of medical devices or Medicare Part B payment rules. *See, e.g.,* Treas. Reg. §§48.4191-2(i)(C), (ii)(C)-(E).
[70] 77 Fed. Reg. at 72931.
[71] *Id.* at 72932.
[72] *See supra* note footnote 22.
[73] 77 Fed. Reg. at 72933.

In: Federal Excise Taxes
Editor: Jerold M. Busch

ISBN: 978-1-62948-483-9

Chapter 4

THE FEDERAL EXCISE TAX ON GASOLINE AND THE HIGHWAY TRUST FUND: A SHORT HISTORY*

James M. Bickley

SUMMARY

Excise taxes have long been a part of our country's revenue history. In the field of gasoline taxation, the states led the way with Oregon enacting the first tax on motor fuels in 1919. By 1932, all states and the District of Columbia had followed suit with tax rates that ranged between two and seven cents per gallon. The federal government first imposed its excise tax on gasoline at a one-cent per gallon rate in 1932. The gas tax was enacted to correct a federal budgetary imbalance. It continued to support general revenue during World War II and the Korean War.

Economists know the gasoline excise tax as a "manufacturer's excise tax" because the government imposes it at production (i.e., the producer, refiner, or importer) for efficiency in collection. Particularly in the short run, when the demand for gasoline is relatively inelastic, economists recognize that any increase in the gasoline tax ultimately falls on the consumer.

The *Highway Revenue Act of 1956* established the federal Highway Trust Fund (HTF) for the direct purpose of funding the construction of an

* This is an edited, reformatted and augmented version of Congressional Research Service, Publication No. RL30304, dated September 7, 2012.

interstate highway system, and aiding in the finance of primary, secondary, and urban routes. Each time Congress has extended the Highway Trust Fund it has also extended the federal excise tax on gasoline.

In the 112th Congress, a series of extensions of the surface transportation legislation have occurred. These extensions reauthorized the federal government's highway, mass transit, and surface transportation safety programs and levied highway user taxes. Extended taxes on gasoline and diesel fuels provided approximately 90% of the funding for the Highway Trust Fund and 80% of the funding for mass transit programs. Other extended taxes were levied on heavy trucks, truck tires, gasohol, and fuel from natural or petroleum gas.

On March 4, 2011, President Obama signed H.R. 662, the *Surface Transportation Extension Act of 2011* (P.L. 112-5). This law extended federal-aid highway, highway safety, motor carrier safety transit, and other programs funded out of the Highway Trust Fund through September 30, 2011. On September 16, 2011, President Obama signed H.R. 2887, *Surface and Air Transportation Programs Extension Act of 2011* (P.L. 112-30), which extended, through March 31, 2012, current surface transportation programs and the motor fuel, heavy truck, and truck tire taxes that support the HTF. On March 30, 2012, President Obama signed H.R. 4281, *Surface Transportation Extension Act of 2012* (P.L. 112-102), which extended the federal surface transportation programs and financing through June 30, 2012. On June 29, 2012, President Obama signed H.R. 6064, *Temporary Surface Transportation Extension Act of 2012* (P.L. 112-140), which extended the surface transportation programs and financing through July 6, 2012. On July 6, 2012, President Obama signed H.R. 4348, *Moving Ahead for Progress in the 21st Century Act* or *Map-21* (P.L. 112-141). This law authorized appropriations for the federal surface transportation programs through October 1, 2014, and financing, including gasoline and diesel taxes, through September 30, 2016. The extended gasoline tax rate was 18.4 cents per gallon and the extended diesel tax rate was 24.4 cents per gallon. These rates include a 0.1 cent per gallon tax levied and deposited in the Leaking Underground Storage Tank (LUST) Trust Fund.

INTRODUCTION

Although excise taxes have long been a source of federal tax revenue, the federal manufacturers excise tax on gasoline was first incorporated into the federal tax structure by the Revenue Act of 1932, which became law on June 6, 1932.[1] A manufacturer's excise tax is one that is collected at the level of production. A tax imposed at the production or importation level provides ease in administration and revenue collection.[2]

Prior to the 1932 act, there had been a reluctance on the part of federal officials and Congress to impose this tax at the federal level. Instead, they preferred to relinquish this revenue source to the states to help them finance their revenue needs. Oregon was the first state to levy a gasoline tax in 1919. As of January 1932, all of the states and the District of Columbia had enacted legislation imposing a tax on gasoline with rates that ranged from two to seven cents per gallon.

However, during the severe depression of the 1930s, federal revenues were sharply reduced and higher expenditures were made for relief and public works programs. As a result, the Secretary of the Treasury, in his annual report for FY1931, reported that the federal government had incurred a budgetary deficit of some $903 million that year. This marked the first year in more than a decade when federal receipts failed to exceed federal expenditures and produce a budgetary surplus. Moreover, the Secretary of the Treasury estimated then that even higher deficits were anticipated in the years immediately following: $2.1 billion in FY1932, and $1.4 billion in FY1933.

Gasoline Excise Tax for Deficit Reduction—1932

To correct this budgetary imbalance, the Secretary of the Treasury submitted comprehensive tax-raising and expenditure-reduction proposals for congressional action. Among the tax recommendations were those for legislation increasing individual and corporation income, estate and gift, excise, and other taxes. Included in the excise tax proposals was the request for a new federal manufacturer's excise tax on gasoline, to be levied at the rate of one cent per gallon and scheduled to end in 1934. It was estimated that adoption of such a tax would yield the U.S. Treasury approximately $165 million in revenues during FY1933.

The House of Representatives, in its consideration of and action on these revenue-raising proposals, initially refused to impose a new federal tax on gasoline. The Senate amended the House-passed bill, however, authorizing a gasoline tax at the rate of one cent per gallon. Congress retained the tax in the final version of the bill approved by the House and Senate conference committee and signed into law.

As approved, Section 617(a) of the Revenue Act of 1932[3] imposed a federal tax on gasoline sold by a producer or importer at the rate of one cent per gallon. Under Section 617(c) of this legislation, the term "producer" included a "refiner, compounder, or blender, and a dealer selling gasoline exclusively to producers of gasoline, as well as a producer." Gasoline was defined to include gasoline, benzyl, and any other liquids used primarily as a fuel to propel motor vehicles, motor boats, or airplanes. Section 629 of this act made this tax effective on June 21, 1932, for a temporary period, with provision for its end just over a year later on June 30, 1933. The *Annual Report of the Commissioner of Internal Revenue* for FY1933 reported that the federal government derived $124.9 million from the excise tax on gasoline. Thus, the gasoline tax represented 7.7% of the total Internal Revenue collection of $1.62 billion derived from all sources during FY1933.

Shortly before the tax was scheduled to expire, Congress approved two bills that extended this tax for an additional year and increased its rate. Under P.L. 73 approved by the 73rd Congress,[4] Congress extended this tax until June 30, 1934. The National Industrial Recovery Act,[5] signed into law on the same day, included provisions governing the rate of this tax. Section 211(a) of this act authorized the increase in federal gasoline tax from one cent to 1.5 cents per gallon, effective June 17, 1933. Section 217(b) provided for this tax to be reduced to one cent per gallon on the first day of the calendar year following the date proclaimed by the President when either of the following occurred: (1) the close of the first fiscal year ending after 1933 when total federal receipts exceeded total federal expenditures, or (2) the repeal of the 18th amendment to the Constitution, establishing national prohibition (repeal would bring in additional revenues to the U.S. Treasury from alcohol taxes).

Subsequently, President Franklin D. Roosevelt proclaimed repeal of the 18th amendment to the Constitution on December 5, 1933. Therefore, under authority of Section 217(b) of the National Industrial Recovery Act, the federal gasoline tax reverted to its former rate of one cent per gallon on January 1, 1934.

Section 603 of the Revenue Act of 1934,[6] approved in the spring of 1934, continued this tax at the rate of one cent per gallon beyond its scheduled expiration date of June 30, 1934.

National Defense Requirements

The one-cent rate was maintained until just before the United States entered World War II, when, as a result of increased national defense requirements, Congress again took action increasing this tax. Section 210 of the Revenue Act of 1940[7] authorized an increase to 1.5 cents per gallon for the five-year period beginning on July 1, 1940, and continuing through June 30, 1945, as part of a defense tax.

The following year, under Section 521(a)(20) of the Revenue Act of 1941,[8] this rate was made permanent by elimination of the June 30, 1945, expiration date that had been specified in the Revenue Act of 1940.

The 1.5-cent per gallon rate continued for more than a decade until the outbreak of the Korean War, when Congress increased the rate to two cents per gallon under authority of Section 489 of the Revenue Act of 1951.[9] This rate became effective on November 1, 1951, and Congress authorized it to continue until March 31, 1954. After this date, Congress scheduled the rate to be reduced to its former rate of 1.5 cents per gallon.

Before this reduction took place, Congress passed the Excise Tax Reduction Act of 1954,[10] and under Section 601(a)(6) of this legislation, the two-cent per gallon rate was extended for an additional year—until March 31, 1955.

During the next two years Congress passed legislation granting one-year extensions of the two-cent per gallon tax on gasoline by approval of the Tax Rate Extension Act of 1955[11] (Section 3(a)(3)) and the Tax Rate Extension Act of 1956[12] (Section 3(a)(3)), which continued the rate first to March 31, 1956, and then to March 31, 1957.

P.L. 466, approved by the 84th Congress,[13] provided that the Treasury Department refund those taxes paid on gasoline used on farms for farming purposes purchased after December 31, 1955.

HIGHWAY TRUST FUND

The Federal Aid Highway Act of 1956[14] provided for a significant expansion in the federal-aid highway program and authorized federal funding over a longer period to permit long-range planning. It was considered necessary to authorize the entire interstate highway program to assure orderly planning and completion of this network of highways throughout the United States as efficiently and as economically as possible. Consequently, this act authorized appropriations for the 13-year period from FY1957 through FY1969 for this highway system. To make the federal aid highway program self-financing, the Highway Revenue Act of 1956[15] was incorporated as Title II of this legislation and imposed new taxes and increased others levied on highway users who directly benefitted from this program.

Section 205 of this Highway Revenue Act authorized an increase in the federal gasoline tax from two to three cents per gallon for the 16-year period from July 1, 1956, through June 30, 1972. After that, the Congress scheduled the tax to be reduced to 1.5 cents per gallon.

Section 209 of this act authorized the creation of the Highway Trust Fund, to which there was to be appropriated from the General Fund of the Treasury certain percentages of receipts derived from highway-user taxes: gasoline, diesel and special motor fuel, tread rubber, tires and inner tubes, trucks, buses, etc. One hundred percent of the federal gasoline tax receipts were transferred to the Highway Trust Fund.

It was argued that transferring such taxes to the Highway Trust Fund was necessary to cover anticipated expenditures to be made under the federal aid highway program for the 16-year period from FY1957 through FY1972. H.Rept. 2022 (84th Congress), issued on this legislation, estimated that highway-user taxes would yield some \$38.5 billion in revenues for this trust fund during this 16-year period—enough to cover anticipated expenditures of approximately \$37.3 billion (during this same period) for the federal aid highway program.

This legislation also arranged for refunding a certain portion of federal gasoline taxes paid that were used for non-highway purposes or by local transit systems.

Since enactment of this legislation, Congress has continued to pass laws extending the life of the Highway Trust Fund and extending and increasing the rates imposed on gasoline.

Under Section 201(a) of the Federal Aid Highway Act of 1959,[16] the federal gasoline tax was increased from three to four cents per gallon, a change that was to be in effect from October 1, 1959, through June 30, 1961.

Under Section 201(b) of the Federal Aid Highway Act of 1961,[17] this four-cent rate was extended beyond June 30, 1961. The scheduled reduction to 1.5 cents per gallon, which the Highway Revenue Act of 1956 had authorized to take place on July 1, 1972, was deferred until October 1, 1972.

Following the 1961 act, the next law affecting the federal gasoline tax was the Federal-Aid Highway Act of 1970.[18] Under Section 303(a)(6) of this act, the scheduled reduction in the rate of this tax to 1.5 cents per gallon was deferred from September 30, 1972, to September 30, 1977.

Again in 1976, an extension of excise tax rates without the scheduled rate reductions allocated to the Highway Trust Fund was provided in Title III of the Federal Aid Highway Act of 1976.[19] The Interstate Highway System was obviously not going to be completed in 1977 (it was estimated in 1976 that it might be completed in 1988). Lack of time to study and report to Congress on modifications to the Highway Trust Fund led to the two-year extension. Congress was concerned that without this legislation funding would be interrupted. Thus, Congress delayed decision-making until it could gather additional information.

Two years later, Congress had not yet decided on modifications to the trust fund and its related taxes. The Ways and Means Committee accepted the recommendation of the Public Works Committee and approved an extension of the trust fund and the taxes payable to the fund. This five-year extension through September 30, 1984, became part of the Surface Transportation Assistance Act of 1978.[20]

Congress gathered extensive information on highway finance and related taxes in 1982. Two major studies were submitted to Congress. The first was a cost allocation study done by the Department of Transportation in May 1982. The second was a study of the excise tax structure that the Department of the Treasury provided to Congress in December 1982. Further, Congress held more than a dozen hearings before the passage of the Surface Transportation Assistance Act of 1982.[21]

The act contains what is commonly called the 4R Program: interstate reconstruction, resurfacing, restoration, and rehabilitation. The completion and selective expansion of the Interstate Highway System remained the primary goals under the bill. Congress raised the gasoline excise tax from its previous level of four cents per gallon to nine cents per gallon. With this increase, Congress eliminated some highway user charges while increasing others. The act also provided that one cent of the five-cent increase in the motor fuel taxes was to be allocated for mass transit purposes. The bill set up a special Mass Transit Account for expenditures made under the Urban Mass Transportation Act of 1964.

In 1986, in response to concerns about the cost for cleanup of leaking underground storage tanks containing petroleum products, Congress established the Leaking Underground Storage Tank Trust Fund.[22] This fund received revenues of 0.1 cent per gallon on the sale or use of gasoline (first effective January 1, 1987). Congress scheduled the tax to expire on the earlier of December 31, 1991, or the last day of the month in which the Secretary of the Treasury estimated that net revenues in the fund were at least $500 million. This additional tax ended after August 31, 1990, because the Leaking Underground Storage Tank Trust Fund had reached its net revenue target for cancellation.[23]

The Surface Transportation and Uniform Relocation Assistance Act of 1987[24] extended the highway-related excise taxes (including the tax on gasoline) through September 30, 1993.

GASOLINE EXCISE TAX FOR DEFICIT REDUCTION

Under provisions of the Omnibus Budget Reconciliation Act of 1990 (OBRA90),[25] the tax rate on highway and motorboat fuels was increased by five cents per gallon. Thus, the tax increased from nine to 14 cents per gallon of gasoline. Half of the increase in revenues from the gasoline tax imposed on highway use vehicles was dedicated as additional funding for the Highway Trust Fund. The remaining half of revenues was deposited in the General Fund and dedicated for federal deficit reduction. Of the 2.5-cent increase dedicated to the Highway Trust Fund, 0.5 cents were dedicated to the Mass Transit Account in that trust fund. Thus, Congress raised the Mass Transit Account funding from one cent to 1.5 cents. OBRA90 also reinstated the Leaking Underground Storage Tank Trust Fund (LUST). The LUST tax recommenced at the same 0.1- cent-per-gallon tax rate.[26] The 14-cent tax rate was scheduled to expire on September 30, 1995, while the LUST tax was scheduled to terminate three months later on December 31, 1995.

The conventional view that had held since the establishment of the Highway Trust Fund, which was that the gasoline tax was a user tax, was challenged. With the passage of OBRA90, the gasoline tax returned to the role it served prior to 1957: a General Fund revenue source, at least in part.

The following year Congress passed the Intermodal Surface Transportation Efficiency Act (ISTEA) of 1991.[27] The revenue title is the Surface Transportation Revenue Act of 1991. This act extended the highway-related excise taxes (including the tax on gasoline in Section 8002(a)(3)) for four years. Hence, this law extended the tax on gasoline (without an increase in tax rate) through September 30, 1999. In addition, under provisions of the act, states were permitted to spend their Highway Trust Fund grants on a broader range of alternative transportation modes and related infrastructure needs. This was done in response to the argument that highway users benefit from expenditures on mass transit and other transportation modes because the availability of these travel alternatives alleviates congestion on existing highways, which in turn reduces the need to build additional roadways.

Also included in provisions of ISTEA was the establishment of a new trust fund known as the National Recreational Trails Trust Fund. This fund receives tax transfers from the Highway Trust Fund that represent tax receipts (imposed on gasoline, diesel, and special motor fuels) collected from *non-highway* recreational fuel use. Examples of recreational fuels are those used in vehicles on recreational trails or back-country terrain, and non-business fuel used in outdoor recreational equipment, such as camp stoves.

Once again, the gasoline excise tax was changed under provisions of the Omnibus Budget Reconciliation Act of 1993 (OBRA93, Section 13241(a)).[28] Under provisions of OBRA93, the additional 2.5-cent gasoline tax dedicated for deficit reduction was transferred to the Highway Trust Fund beginning October 1, 1995. This additional 2.5-cent tax rate was extended from October 1, 1995, to September 30, 1999. The highway portion of the fund receives two cents, while the Mass Transit Account is credited with 0.5 cent of the increased funding. In addition, OBRA93 provided for a permanent, additional 4.3 cents per gallon tax on gasoline starting on October 1, 1993. Thus, the combination of the 2.5-cents OBRA90 gasoline tax rate and the permanent 4.3-cent OBRA93 gasoline tax rate resulted in a total of 6.8 cents per gallon dedicated to deficit reduction purposes between October 1, 1993, and October 1, 1995. Revenues collected from this 6.8-cent portion of the tax were placed in the General Fund of the U.S. Treasury.

As previously related, provisions of OBRA90 terminated the LUST tax rate of 0.1 cent on December 31, 1995. Thus, the 18.3-cent federal gasoline excise tax rate was in effect from January 1, 1996, to October 1, 1997, before increasing to 18.4 cents with the reintroduction of the LUST tax. This 18.3-cent rate includes the permanent 4.3 cents initially dedicated to federal deficit reduction but which now goes to the Highway Trust Fund.

Reversion from Deficit Reduction to User Tax Status

During the early months of 1996, the price of gasoline at the pump was rising and a renewed interest developed in federal gasoline excise taxes. Three principal views developed. The first view was that the 4.3 cents increase in federal excise taxes imposed under OBRA93 should be repealed. Proponents of repeal argued that the 4.3 cents repeal could lead to a similar reduction in gasoline pump prices. Two camps developed which supported retaining the tax. Some supporters of the tax expressed the view that while the 4.3-cent tax should be retained, the tax revenues should be returned to the Highway Trust

Fund for long-term capital improvements. They argued for increased funding of the nation's highway infrastructure. Others expressed the view that the monies should continue to be collected and used for deficit reduction. This camp of supporters argued that the gasoline price increase was temporary and that over the long term prices would trend lower. Partially in response to this debate, the chairman of the House Ways and Means Committee, Representative Bill Archer, appointed a bi-partisan group to examine the tax treatment of each of the transportation modes with a goal of rationalizing the current myriad tax rules applying to the transportation sector.

Included in the Taxpayer Relief Act of 1997[29] was a provision that returns the General Fund portion of the tax back to the Highway Trust Fund. This provision, first added by a Senate amendment (and modified in conference), provides that the 4.3-cent tax is divided between the Highway Account (3.45 cents) and the Mass Transit Account (0.85 cent). The provision was effective on October 1, 1997. Thus, of the total 18.3 cents dedicated to the Highway Trust Fund, 15.44 cents goes to the Highway Account and 2.86 cents to the Mass Transit Account.[30] As a consequence, the disposition of revenues was altered by the act so that all revenues now accrue to the Highway Trust Fund and none are applied to deficit reduction. Consumers experienced no price change due to enactment of this provision since the federal tax rate on gasoline remained the same.

In addition, the Taxpayer Relief Act of 1997 reinstated the Leaking Underground Storage Tank Trust Fund excise tax, which had expired January 1, 1996.[31] The tax was reinstated at its prior tax rate of 0.1 cent per gallon on all types of motor fuels. The tax rate change was effective from October 1, 1997, through March 31, 2005.[32] The LUST excise tax was then extended for an additional seven months (through September 30, 2005).[33] Under a provision contained in the Energy Policy Act of 2005 the LUST tax is extended through September 30, 2011. The imposition of the gasoline tax is codified under IRC Section 4081.

Although the component of the federal gasoline tax formerly (but no longer) applied to deficit reduction continues without an expiration date, the 14 cents scheduled to expire on September 30, 1999, has been extended. Congress not only extended the gasoline excise tax but also the other highway-related excise taxes. The House had proposed to extend the heavy truck tire tax until October 1, 2000, whereupon it would expire. However, in conference with the Senate, all the highway-related excise taxes were extended through September 30, 2005. The legislative vehicle for this extension was the Transportation Equity Act for the 21st Century[34] generally known as TEA-21.

The revenue portion of this act (Title IX) was titled the Surface Transportation Revenue Act of 1998.

This act also provided that the Highway Trust Fund no longer earns interest on unspent balances (effective September 30, 1998). The balance of funds that exceed $8 billion in the Highway Account was canceled on October 1, 1998. In addition, TEA-21 provided that the National Recreational Trails Trust Fund established under ISTEA be repealed. In the absence of an appropriation of funds, no revenues had been available for expenditure. The conference agreement noted that similar expenditure purposes are provided by authorized amounts from the Highway Trust Fund.

Beginning in the 108th Congress, a series of laws were passed extending the funding for Highway Trust Fund. These extensions during the 108th-111th Congresses are described in the Appendix.

EXTENSIONS IN THE 112TH CONGRESS

In the 112th Congress, a series of extensions of the surface transportation legislation have occurred. These extensions reauthorized the federal government's highway, mass transit, and surface transportation safety programs and levied user taxes. Extended taxes on gasoline and diesel fuels provided approximately 90% of the funding for the Highway Trust Fund and 80% of the funding for mass transit programs.[35] Other extended taxes were levied on heavy trucks, truck tires, gasohol, and fuel from natural or petroleum gas.

For FY2011, the Congressional Budget Office estimated that revenues and interest credited to the Highway Trust Fund will total $36.9 billion, which was divided into the Highway Account ($31.8 billion) and the Mass Transit Account ($5.1 billion).[36] The three primary revenue sources were the gasoline tax ($24.0 billion), the diesel tax ($8.7 billion), and the tax on trucks and trailers ($2.2 billion).[37] The tax on trucks and trailers would only finance highways.

On March 4, 2011,President Obama signed H.R. 662, the *Surface Transportation Extension Act of 2011* (P.L. 112-5). This law extended federal-aid highway, highway safety, motor carrier safety transit, and other programs funded out of the Highway Trust Fund through September 30, 2011.

On May 17, 2011, the Senate Finance Committee held a hearing on the "Highway Trust Fund and Paying for Highways." Joseph Kile, Assistant Director for Microeconomic Studies at CBO, testified:

> The law that authorizes collection of taxes for and spending from the Highway Trust Fund is set to expire on September 30, 2011. Even if the provisions of that law are extended, the trust fund will be unable to meet its obligations in a timely manner by the summer or fall of 2012, CBO projects, unless transfers similar to those in the past are made, other sources of revenue are identified, or spending is reduced.[38]

Different options for financing highways were examined.[39]

On July 13, 2011, Representative Mica, chairman of the House Transportation and Infrastructure Committee, sent a letter to the U.S. Chamber of Commerce opposing the chamber's support for a gasoline tax increase.[40] In his letter, he stated:

> The reaction from National Chamber of Commerce representatives to the rollout of the Republican Surface Transportation Reauthorization outline was most disappointing and a potential setback to enacting a long term transportation reauthorization. During my years of service on the Transportation and Infrastructure Committee I have seen the National Chamber of Commerce evolve from an Association that would advocate strong infrastructure and responsible fiscal policy on behalf of its members to an organization whose primary purpose in the national infrastructure arena appears to be to lead the lobby for tax increases.[41]

Representative John Mica and Senator Barbara Boxer, chairwoman of the Senate Environment and Public Works Committee, proposed long-term highway bills, which had substantial differences.[42]

On August 31, 2011, President Obama called on Congress to pass a clean extension of funding for the surface transportation law.[43] In response, Representative John L. Mica issued a press release that stated:

> Republicans have offered positive and financially responsible alternatives to get these measures moving. As Chairman of the House Transportation Committee, I will agree to one additional highway program extension, this being the eighth of the overdue transportation reauthorization.[44]

On September 13, 2011, the House approved H.R. 2887, *Surface Air Transportation Programs Act of 2011*, which extended through March 31, 2012, current surface transportation programs and the motor fuel, heavy truck, and truck tire taxes that support the Highway Trust Fund.[45] On September 15, 2011, the Senate approved H.R. 2887.[46] On September 16, 2011, President Obama signed H.R. 2887, P.L. 112-30.[47]

On October 31, 2011, Senator Amy Klobuchar introduced the *Rebuild America Jobs Act* (S. 1769). This bill included $50 billion for road, transit, rail, and aviation investments and $10 billion for the creation of a national infrastructure bank.[48] The bill proposed a 0.7% surcharge on households earning more than $1 million per year. On November 2, 2011, Senator Orrin Hatch introduced S. 1786, *Long-Term Surface Transportation Extension Act of 2011*, which would extend for two years Highway Trust Fund expenditure authority and highway-related taxes and rescind unspent federal funds to offset revenue losses.[49] On November 3, 2011, both S. 1769 and S. 1786 failed to obtain the 60 vote procedural threshold necessary for further consideration in the Senate.[50]

On November 4, 2011, Senators Barbara Boxer and James Inhofe introduced a two-year reauthorization of U.S. surface transportation programs at current funding levels, *Moving Ahead for Progress in the 21st Century Act* or (*MAP-21*).[51] This bill would also have made make substantial changes to the structure, formulas, and funding distribution of the federal highway program. On November 9, 2011, the Senate Environment and Public Works Committee marked up and reported favorable on the highway provisions of S. 1813, the *Moving Ahead for Progress in the 21st Century Act* (MAP-21). By February 7, 2012, all committees of jurisdiction had marked up their titles. On March 1, 2012, these titles were folded into S.Amdt. 1761 to S. 1813. On March 5, 2012, in response to a request from Senate Majority Leader Harry Reid, the Congressional Budget Office (CBO) issued estimates for S. 1813, MAP-21, with S.Amdt. 1761. CBO estimated that implementing the bill would have discretionary costs of $47.0 billion over the FY2012-FY2017 period. In addition, CBO estimated that implementing the provisions of the bill for the remainder of FY2012 and for FY2013 would result in an end-of-year balance in 2013 of approximately $2 billion in the highway account of the Highway Trust Fund and about $3 billion in the transit account of the Highway Trust Fund.[52]

On March 30, 2012, President Obama signed H.R. 4281, *Surface Transportation Extension Act of 2012* (P.L. 112-102), which extended the federal surface transportation programs and financing through June 30, 2012. On June 29, 2012, President Obama signed H.R. 6064, *Temporary Surface Transportation Extension Act of 2012* (P.L. 112-140), which extended the surface transportation programs and financing through July 6, 2012. On July 6, 2012, President Obama signed H.R. 4348, *Moving Ahead for Progress in the 21st Century Act* or *Map-21* (P.L. 112-141). This law authorized appropriations for the federal surface transportation programs through October 1, 2014, and financing, including gasoline and diesel taxes, through September 30, 2016. The extended gasoline tax rate was 18.4 cents per gallon and the extended diesel tax rate was 24.4 cents per gallon. These rates include a 0.1 cent per gallon tax levied and deposited in the Leaking Underground Storage Tank (LUST) Trust Fund.

ISSUES

In economic theory, there are two principles often cited for determining how the burden of a tax ought to be distributed. The first is the ability-to-pay principle, which suggests that a tax ought to be positively related to an individual's economic welfare.

The second principle, the benefit principle, suggests the burden should relate to an individual's return from the government good or service funded by the tax. Currently, an excise tax on gasoline seems to most closely follow the benefits principle. In fact, the excise tax has commonly been referred to as a "user fee." However, this is not the only economic rationale that could be forwarded in support of a gasoline tax. Some argue that gasoline taxes, and energy taxes, more generally, can be imposed to influence behavior, specifically as a mechanism to reduce, or internalize the costs of, social and environmental externalities such as congestion and pollution.[53]

The economic benefits derived from the expenditure of funds for transportation infrastructure, while important to the analysis, are distinct from the associated costs and benefits related to the method of raising the necessary revenues.

Particularly in the short run, when the demand for gasoline is relatively inelastic, economists recognize any increase in the gasoline tax is generally passed forward to consumers in the form of higher prices. As consumers modify their behaviors to respond to the increase in price (depending upon the magnitude), economic theory would predict consumers would purchase less gasoline, all else being equal. As a result, producers and retailers may not be able to pass on the entire magnitude of the tax to consumers. Although consumers would likely bear the majority of the excise tax increase on gasoline, producers may have lower net revenues and, thus, share some portion of the burden. See Table 1 for a complete summary of the gasoline tax rate changes.

Table 1. Summary of Changes in the Rate of the Federal Manufacturers' Excise Tax on Gasoline

Rate of Tax (in cents per gallon)	Period to Which Applicable
1	June 21, 1932, to June 16, 1933
1.5	June 17, 1933, to December 31, 1933
1	January 1, 1934, to June 30, 1940
1.5	July 1, 1940, to October 31, 1951
2	November 1, 1951, to June 30, 1956
3	July 1, 1956, to September 30, 1959
4	October 1, 1959, to March 31, 1983
9	April 1, 1983, to December 31, 1986
9.1	January 1, 1987, to August 31, 1990a
9	September 1, 1990, to November 30, 1990
14.1	December 1, 1990, to September 30, 1993
18.4	October 1, 1993, to December 31, 1995b
18.3	January 1, 1996,c to September 30, 1997
18.4	October 1, 1997,d to September 30, 2016
4.3	November 1, 2016, and thereafter

Source: Prepared by the Congressional Research Service.

[a] This act provided that the 0.1-cent per gallon tax will terminate on the earlier of December 31, 1991, or when the Secretary of the Treasury determines that taxes equivalent to at least $500 million in net revenues are in the Trust Fund. This additional tax terminated after August 31, 1990, because the LUST Trust Fund had reached its net revenue target for termination. (Internal Revenue Service Announcement 90-82, released June 27, 1990.)

[b] Beginning on October 1, 1995, the revenues collected from the 2.5-cent "deficit reduction" rate are to be credited to the account of the Highway Trust Fund. Thus, while the gasoline excise tax rate holds constant at 18.4 cents, the distribution of amounts collected from the gasoline excise tax changes. The Highway Trust Fund will receive increased revenues as the rate credited to that fund increases from 11.5 to 14 cents. At this same time, the amount credited to the General Fund decreases from 6.8 to 4.3 cents.

[c] Pursuant to provisions of OBRA90, the LUST tax terminated on December 31, 1995.

[d] Beginning on October 1, 1997, the *Taxpayer Relief Act of 1997* provides that amounts previously dedicated for deficit reduction be redirected to the Highway Trust Fund through March 31, 2005. Additionally, the LUST tax which had terminated on December 31, 1996, was re-authorized for the period October 1, 1997, through March 31, 2005. A seven month extension (P.L. 109-6) extended the gasoline tax through September 30, 2011. Passage of the *Energy Policy Act of 2005* extended the LUST financing tax rate. On March 4, 2011, President Obama signed H.R. 662, *Surface Transportation Extension Act of 2011* (P.L. 112-5). This law extended the gasoline tax through September 30, 2011. On September 16, 2011, President Obama signed H.R. 2887, *Surface and Air Transportation Programs Extension Act of 2011* (P.L. 112-30), which extended the gasoline tax until March 31, 2012. On March 30, 2011, President Obama signed H.R. 4281, *Surface Transportation Extension Act of 2012* (P.L. 112-102), which extended the gasoline tax through June 30, 2012. On June 29, 2012, President Obama signed H.R. 6064, *Temporary Surface Transportation Extension Act of 2012* (P.L. 112-140), which extended the gasoline tax through July 6, 2012. On July 6, 2012, President Obama signed H.R. 4348, *Moving Ahead for Progress in the 21st Century Act* or *Map-21* (P.L. 112-141). This law extended the gasoline tax through September 30, 2016.

Appendix. Extensions of Funding for the Highways Trust Fund: 108th-111th Congresses

Extensions in the 108th Congress

Lawmakers first enacted the Surface Transportation Extension Act of 2003 (P.L. 108-88), which was a short-term extension of the highway, highway safety, motor carrier safety, transit, and other programs funded out of the Highway Trust Fund. The five-month extension was signed into law by President Bush September 30, 2003. Four additional short-term extensions were enacted after the expiration of this initial extension. The Surface Transportation Extension Act of 2004 became P.L. 108-202 in February 2004. Part III of the Surface Transportation Extension Act of 2004, P.L. 108-263, was enacted in June 2004, and Part IV of the act, P.L. 108-280, became law at the end of July 2004. The Surface Transportation Extension Act of 2004, Part V became P.L. 108-310 and provided extensions through May 31, 2005, for those programs authorized by the Transportation Equity Act for the 21st Century (TEA-21). This last extension provided $31.8 billion in contract authority, of which $2.7 billion was for FY2004 and $29.1 billion was available for the eight-month period from October 1, 2004, through May 31, 2005. Under provisions of the Transportation Equity Act for the 21st Century, expenditures from the trust fund would have ceased if Congress had failed to approve these short-term extensions.[54]

The revenue sources for the Highway Trust Fund include six different excise taxes, which are taxes on the highway motor fuels, gasoline, diesel fuel, and kerosene; a retail sales tax on heavy highway vehicles; a manufacturers' excise tax on heavy vehicle tires;[55] and an annual use tax on heavy vehicles. These excises were not affected by the temporary extensions, since under the law at that time the excise taxes were not scheduled for expiration until September 30, 2005.

Extensions in the 109th Congress

The 109th Congress initially had until Memorial Day to complete work on the new highway bill. That extension included language that provided for the 2.5 cents per gallon tax on ethanol to be deposited into the Highway Trust Fund for one year. Those monies had previously been deposited into the general fund. That change was estimated to generate $940 million in new revenue for the Highway Trust Fund. Also included was a one-year extension of the budgetary fire walls that tie gas tax revenue to highway and transit programs, while at the same time waiving for one year the Byrd self-solvency test for the trust fund and releasing the $716 million the Federal Highway Administration was holding onto as a result of the trust funds failure of that test. Further, the extension "also included a new 'supplemental minimum guarantee' program that was designed to ensure that all states continue to receive their 90.5% minimum guaranteed rate of return on fuel taxes sent to the Highway Trust Fund."[56]

Again in the 109th Congress, it was necessary to pass a number of extensions so that the Highway Trust Fund could continue operations until enactment of a longer term re-authorizing measure. Accordingly, these extensions were known as the Surface Transportation Extension Acts of 2005.[57]

Just prior to the summer recess, Congress sent legislation (H.R. 3) to the President which extended trust fund expenditures through FY2009 and continued the highway related taxes through FY2011. The legislation also included provisions aimed at stopping fuel fraud, provided tax-exempt financing authority to finance highway projects and rail-truck transfer facilities, and modified a number of excise taxes (both highway and non-highway related). President Bush signed the Safe, Accountable, Flexible, Efficient Transportation Equity Act: A Legacy for Users (SAFETEA-LU) (the "Highway Act") into law on August 10, 2005. The act extended for six years the Highway Trust Fund excise taxes due to expire in 2005 until 2011. All of the excise taxes, including the federal excise tax on gasoline, were continued at the prior tax rates. The act established the Motor Fuel Tax Enforcement Advisory Commission, which was scheduled to terminate on September 30, 2009. In other legislation, the Energy Policy Act of 2005 extended the Leaking Underground Storage Tank (LUST) Trust Fund financing rate for the same six-year period that the highway excise taxes were extended. Thus, the LUST tax will expire after September 30, 2011.

Extensions in the 110th Congress

At the time of passage of SAFETEA-LU, tax changes, the unexpended balance in the trust fund and economic growth were expected to provide sufficient financing for the Highway Trust Fund. But shortfalls developed which required general fund contributions.[58] On September 15, 2008, P.L. 110-318, *To Amend the Internal Revenue Code of 1986 to Restore the Highway Trust Fund Balance*, was passed. This law transferred $8.017 billion from the U.S. Treasury to the Highway Trust Fund, which provided financing through the end of FY2008.

Extensions in the 111th Congress

According to the Congressional Budget Office,

> In 2010, the Hiring Incentives to Restore Employment Act (P.L. 111-147) authorized the most recent transfer from the general fund and the resumption of interest credits to the trust fund. That law also shifted certain refunds for tax-exempt use of motor fuels, such as fuel consumed by state and local governments, from being paid out of the Highway Trust Fund to being paid out of the general fund, also boosting trust fund balances. Because of the infusion of general revenues, at the end of 2010, the account balances were positive.[59]

On December 22, 2010, the *Continuing Appropriations and Surface Transportation Extension Act, 2011* (H.R. 3082) became P.L. 111-322. This law extended SAFETEA-LU authorization of appropriations out of the Highway Trust Fund through March 4, 2011.

End Notes

1 The author updated this report, which was previously written by Pamela J. Jackson.

2 For an analysis of the economic effects of a change in the amount of the gasoline tax, see CRS Report R40808, *The Role of Federal Gasoline Excise Taxes in Public Policy*, by Robert Pirog.

3 Revenue Act of 1932, P.L. 154, 72nd Congress, approved June 6, 1932.

4 Act to Extend the Gasoline Tax for One Year, to Modify Postage Rates on Mail Matter and for other Purposes, P.L. 73, 73rd Congress, approved June 16, 1933.

5 National Industrial Recovery Act, P.L. 67, 73rd Congress, approved June 16, 1933.

6 Revenue Act of 1934, P.L. 216, 73rd Congress, approved May 10, 1934.

7 Revenue Act of 1940, P.L. 656, 76th Congress, approved June 25, 1940.

8 Revenue Act of 1941, P.L. 250, 77th Congress, approved September 20, 1941.

9 Revenue Act of 1951, P.L. 183, 82d Congress, approved October 20, 1951.

10 Excise Tax Reduction Act of 1954, P.L. 324, 83rd Congress, approved March 31, 1954.

11 Tax Rate Extension Act of 1955, P.L. 18, 84th Congress, approved March 30, 1955.

12 Tax Rate Extension Act of 1956, P.L. 458, 84th Congress, approved March 29, 1956.

[13] Act to Amend the Internal Revenue Code of 1954 to Relieve Farmers from Excise Taxes in the Case of Gasoline and Special Fuels Used on Farms for Farming Purposes, P.L. 266, 84th Congress, approved April 1 2, 1956.

[14] Federal-Aid Highway and Highway Revenue Act of 1956, P.L. 627, 84th Congress, approved June 29, 1956.

[15] Ibid.

[16] Federal-Aid Highway Act of 1959, P.L. 86-342, approved September 21, 1959.

[17] Federal-Aid Highway Act of 1961, P.L. 87-61, approved June 29, 1961.

[18] Federal-Aid Highway Act of 1970, P.L. 91-605, approved December 31, 1970.

[19] Federal-Aid Highway Act of 1976, P.L. 94-280, approved May 5, 1976.

[20] Surface Transportation Assistance Act of 1978, P.L. 95-599, approved November 6, 1978.

[21] Surface Transportation Assistance Act of 1982, P.L. 97-424, approved January 6, 1983.

[22] Superfund Revenue Act of 1986, P.L. 99-499, approved October 17, 1986.

[23] Internal Revenue Service Announcement 90-82, released June 27, 1990.

[24] Surface Transportation and Uniform Relocation Assistance Act of 1987, P.L. 100-17, approved April 2, 1987.

[25] Omnibus Budget Reconciliation Act of 1990, P.L. 101-508, approved November 5, 1990.

[26] This act also instituted a new 2.5-cent per gallon tax on fuels used in rail transportation effective on December 1, 1990. Rail transportation generally uses diesel fuel. All revenues from this new tax go to general fund revenues with the tax scheduled to expire on October 1, 1995.

[27] Intermodal Surface Transportation Efficiency Act (ISTEA) of 1991, P.L. 102-240, approved December 18, 1991.

[28] Omnibus Budget Reconciliation Act of 1993, P.L. 103-66, approved August 10, 1993.

[29] Taxpayer Relief Act of 1997, P.L. 105-34, approved August 5, 1997.

[30] A technical correction contained in the Transportation Equity Act for the 21st Century (discussed later in this report) provides that deposits are to be equal to 2.86 cents per gallon rather than the 2.85 cents provided in the 1997 Act.

[31] Ibid.

[32] For additional information and a discussion of the LUST tax, see CRS Report RS21201, *Leaking Underground Storage Tanks (USTs): Prevention and Cleanup*, by Mary Tiemann.

[33] Extension of the Leaking Underground Storage Tank Trust Fund Financing Rate, P.L. 109-6, approved March 31, 2005.

[34] Transportation Equity Act for the 21st Century, P.L. 105-178, approved June 9, 1998.

[35] Detailed information about some of this legislation is available in CRS Report R42445, *Surface Transportation Reauthorization Legislation in the 112th Congress: MAP-21, H.R. 7, and H.R. 4348—Major Provisions*, coordinated by Robert S. Kirk.

[36] Ibid., p. 4.

[37] Ibid.

[38] Ibid., p. 1.

[39] Nicola M. White, "Finance Committee Seeks Ways to Fund Transportation Infrastructure," *Tax Notes*, May 23, 2011, p. 797. For an examination of different possible revenue sources for surface transportation infrastructure, see CRS Report R41490, *Surface Transportation Funding and Finance*, by Robert S. Kirk and William J. Mallett.

[40] Adam Snider, "U.S. Chamber's Support for Gas Tax Hike Imperils Surface Transport Bill," Mica Says, *Daily Tax Report*, August 19, 2011, p. G3.

[41] Representative John L. Mica, letter to Thomas J. Donohue, President and CEO of the U.S. Chamber of Commerce, July 13, 2011.

[42] Keith Laing and Bernie Becker, "Gas Tax Issue Could Be Next Political Fight in Congress," *The Hill*, vol. 18, no. 118, August 10, 2011, p. 4.
[43] Michael M. Gleeson, "Obama Calls for Clean Extension of Highway, Aviation Authorization and Taxes," *Tax Notes Today*, September 1, 2011, pp. 1-2.
[44] John Mica, *Statement on President's Transportation Remarks*, Press Release, August 31, 2011, p. 1.
[45] Adam Snider, "House Passes Transportation Stopgap But Coburn Could Slow Senate Floor Action," *Daily Report for Executives*, September 14, 2011, p. A18.
[46] Adam Snider, "Senate OKs Transportation Policy Stopgap After Promise for Long-Term FAA Measure," *Daily Report for Executives*, September 16, 2011, p. A27.
[47] Adam Snider, "Obama Signs Highway, FAA Stopgap Bill, Avoiding Lapse in Aviation, Motor Fuel Taxes," *Daily Report For Executives*, September 19, 2011, p. G5.
[48] Christine Grimaldi, "Democrats' Infrastructure Bill with Surtax, GOP Alternative Fail to Advance in Senate," *Daily Tax Report*, November 4, 2011, p. G6.
[49] "Hatch Bill Would Extend Highway Trust Fund, Highway Taxes," *Tax Notes Today*, November 3, 2011, p.1.
[50] Christine Grimaldi, "Democrats' Infrastructure Bill With Surtax, GOP Alternative Fail To Advance in Senate," p. G6.
[51] "Senators Boxer, Inhofe Unveil Surface Transportation Reauthorization Bill," *Daily Report for Executives*, November 4, 2011, p. 1.
[52] Congressional Budget Office, Letter to Honorable Harry Reid about cost estimates for S. 1813, March 5, 2012, p. 1.
[53] In economics, an externality arises when either the production or consumption of a good or service results in an indirect cost or benefit, which is not reflected in market prices.
[54] For an additional historical perspective on extension legislation, see CRS Report RS21621, *Surface Transportation and Aviation Extension Legislation: A Historical Perspective*, by John W. Fischer and Robert S. Kirk.
[55] The American Jobs Creation Act of 2004 (P.L. 108-357) replaced the tax on tires from one based on tire weight to a tax based on tire load capacity. This legislation also added definitions of "taxable tires," "bias ply tires," and "super single tires." Additional clarification of the definition for "super single tires" was provided with passage of the Energy Policy Act of 2005.
[56] Heather M. Rothman, "Highway Funding Extension Bill Cleared, With Provisions for AMT Relief, Expensing," *Daily Tax Report*, October 1, 2004, No. 190, p. G-11.
[57] Surface Transportation Extension Act of 2005, Part I, P.L. 109-14, approved May 31, 2005. Part II, P.L. 109-20, approved July 1, 2005. Part III, P.L. 109-35, approved July 20, 2005. Part IV, P.L. 109-37, approved July 22, 2005. Part V, P.L. 109-40, approved July 28, 2005. Part VI, P.L. 109-42, approved July 30, 2005.
[58] CRS Report R41490, *Surface Transportation Funding and Finance*, by Robert S. Kirk and William J. Mallett, p. 2.
[59] Congressional Budget Office, *The Highway Trust Fund and Paying for Highways*, Statement of Joseph Kile, Assistant Director for Microeconomic Studies, before the Senate Committee on Finance, May 17, 2011, p. 7.

In: Federal Excise Taxes
Editor: Jerold M. Busch
ISBN: 978-1-62948-483-9

Chapter 5

THE RUM EXCISE TAX COVER-OVER: LEGISLATIVE HISTORY AND CURRENT ISSUES*

Steven Maguire

SUMMARY

Under current law, the excise tax on rum is $13.50 per proof gallon and is collected on rum produced in or imported into the United States. Through 2011, $13.25 per proof gallon of imported rum is transferred or "covered over" to the Treasuries of Puerto Rico (PR) and the United States Virgin Islands (USVI). In FY2011, PR received over $449.0 million in revenue and the USVI received over $133.5 million. The law does not impose any restrictions on how PR and USVI can use the transferred revenues. Both territories use some portion of the revenue to promote and assist the rum industry.

The cover-over provisions for rum extend as far back as 1917 for PR and 1954 for USVI. Recently, the United States Virgin Islands has dedicated a larger share of current and future covered-over revenue to help finance public and private infrastructure that would directly benefit the rum industry.

In the 112th Congress, legislation has been introduced to expand federal control over the use of covered-over revenue. Passage of H.R.

---

* This is an edited, reformatted and augmented version of Congressional Research Service, Publication No. R41028, dated September 20, 2012.

1883 (or similar legislation, S. 986) would result in limits on Puerto Rico's and the USVI's ability to use covered-over revenue to subsidize the rum industry in the islands. The legislation is likely in response to the recent economic development initiatives in the USVI financed in part by rum cover-over revenue. The President's FY2013 budget proposal includes an extension of the $13.25 cover-over, as does S. 3521.

This report provides a history and analysis of the rum cover-over program and current legislative efforts to modify the program. The congressional debate on this legislation could also lead to debate on the broader issue of the cover-over program more generally.

INTRODUCTION

Most federal excise taxes do not apply in the United States Virgin Islands (USVI) and Puerto Rico (PR) or the other possessions. An exception, however, is provided by Section 7652 of the Internal Revenue Code, which applies a special excise tax to items produced in PR or the USVI and shipped to the United States. The tax is equal to any excise tax that would apply to an identical item produced in one of the 50 states or the District of Columbia. The tax was first imposed to ensure that producers in the possessions would not have a tax advantage over goods produced in the United States that are subject to excise taxes.[1]

For example, rum that is produced in either the USVI or PR and that is sold in the states is subject to the same tax as rum produced in the states. Most of the revenue from the so-called equalization tax, however, is returned ("covered over") by the federal government to the treasuries of PR and the USVI.[2] In addition, the Caribbean Basin Economic Recovery Act of 1983 (P.L. 98-67) provides that all revenue from federal excise taxes on rum imported into the United States from any source—including any foreign country—is remitted to the treasuries of PR and the USVI.[3]

The cover-over provisions for rum extend as far back as 1917 for PR and 1954 for the USVI. The covered-over revenue has never been designated for particular purposes by Congress.[4] The territories have tended to dedicate some portion to fund marketing campaigns for the rum industry and general economic development. Annual cover-over revenues in FY2011 were $449.0 million for PR and $133.5 million for the USVI.[5]

In the 112th Congress, legislation has been introduced to expand federal control over the use of covered-over revenue. Passage of H.R. 1883 (or similar legislation, S. 986) would result in limits on Puerto Rico's and the USVI's ability to finance economic development projects with this revenue source. The legislation is likely in response to recent economic development initiatives in the USVI financed in part by rum cover-over revenue. The congressional debate on this legislation could also lead to debate on the broader issue of the cover-over program more generally. In contrast, S. 3521 would simply extend the $13.25 cover-over through 2013.

HISTORY OF THE RUM COVER-OVER

Congress initiated the principles behind the rum cover-over program for Puerto Rico under the Jones Act of 1917, even though, ironically, the same legislation prohibited the production and sale of alcohol. The act stipulated, "providing that hereafter all taxes collected under the internal revenue laws of the United States on articles produced in Porto Rico [sic] and transported to the United States, or consumed in the island shall be covered over into the treasury of Porto Rico [sic]."[6] The House and Senate report language accompanying the Jones Act of 1917 both stated "it is believed to be just and fair that it [Puerto Rico] should receive the internal-revenue taxes collected upon its products, whether those products are used in Porto Rico [sic] or produced in Porto Rico [sic] and transported to and used in the United States."[7] Importantly, there is no mention of congressional intent with regard to spending of such covered-over revenue.

The Revised Organic Act of 1954 (P.L. 83-517) extended the rum cover-over program to the USVI; following is the relevant legislative language:[8]

> There shall be transferred and paid over to the government of the Virgin Islands from the amounts so determined a sum equal to the total amount of revenue collected by the government of the Virgin Islands during the fiscal year, as certified by the Government Comptroller of the Virgin Islands. The money so transferred and paid over shall constitute a separate fund in the treasury of the Virgin Islands and may be expended as the legislature may determine....

The next clause in the legislative language does provide that the President of the United States or his designated representative must approve of such expenditures before the cover-over revenue is obligated.

In the Senate report language accompanying the Revised Organic Act of 1954, Congress expressed a desire that the USVI use the covered-over revenue to loosen the dependence of the USVI on periodic appropriations from the

U.S. government. According to the report language, under a cover-over system, "the people of the Virgin Islands would have a far greater degree of control over their finances than under the present system."[9] The report continues, recommending that "the people of the Virgin Islands bend their efforts to stimulating and increasing business in every way possible."[10] Again, Congress does not outline specific uses for the covered-over revenue. That same year, two rum manufacturers began production in the USVI, Cruzan VIRAL Ltd., and Brugal.[11]

As noted earlier, the Caribbean Basin Economic Recovery Act of 1983 (P.L. 98-67) provides that all revenue from federal excise taxes on rum imported into the United States from any source— including any other foreign country—is to be remitted to the treasuries of PR and the USVI. This provision increased the amount covered over to PR by 17.0% in FY2009 and to the USVI by 7.8% in FY2011.[12] The formula for dividing the "other" revenue between the USVI and PR is complicated but is roughly based on the relative market share of rum each possession produces.

In the report language accompanying the act, Congress clarified that "the bill does not impose restrictions on the uses to which the Government of the Virgin Islands or the Government of Puerto Rico may put the revenues they receive under this provision."[13] The law also stipulates that the *PR share* of excise tax on other rum shall not exceed 87.626889% and not fall below 51%. Accordingly, the *USVI share* cannot drop below 12.373111% or exceed 49%.[14] The floors are important because even if all rum production were to leave Puerto Rico or the USVI for another country, the possessions would still receive a significant share of cover-over revenue from "other" revenue as under the formula in P.L. 98-67. However, if production shifts between the two possessions, the "losing" possession would lose all of the revenue generated by the relocated rum production. Thus, the possession losing the rum producer would be better off if the rum producer relocated outside of PR, USVI, or the United States.

The Deficit Reduction Act of 1984 (P.L. 98-369) placed a cap on the rebate of excise taxes on rum and other distilled spirits. The 1984 act increased the federal tax rate on spirits from $10.50 per proof-gallon to $12.50; subsequent legislation increased the rate to $13.50 per proof-gallon.[15] The 1984 act also provided, however, that the rebate to PR and the USVI would be calculated based on prior law's $10.50 rate. In imposing the cap, Congress stated that it did not wish to expand the rebate (as would have occurred automatically with the tax-rate increase) until it had addressed the question of whether the rebates were proper, given that similar cover-overs were not made to the 50 states.[16]

The Omnibus Budget Reconciliation Act of 1993 (OBRA93; P.L. 103-66) temporarily increased the cap to $11.30 per proof-gallon, effective for shipments of rum and distilled spirits brought into the United States during the five-year period October 1, 1993, through September 30, 1998. The increase was enacted in the context of a scaling-back by the act of the possessions tax credit.

With the expiration of OBRA93's temporary increase in the rebate's cap, the limitation returned to its previous $10.50 level. The Ticket to Work and Work Incentives Improvement Act of 1999 (P.L. 106-170) and the Job Creation and Worker Assistance Act of 2002 (P.L. 107-147), however, provided temporary increases in the cap to $13.25 per proof-gallon through December 31, 2003. In conjunction with the extension of a number of other tax provisions not related to the possessions, the Working Families Tax Relief Act of 2004 (P.L. 108-311) extended the $13.25 amount through 2005. The Tax Relief and Health Care Act of 2006 (P.L. 109-432) extended the $13.25 amount through 2007. On October 3, 2008, the Tax Extenders and Alternative Minimum Tax Relief Act of 2008 (P.L. 110-343) extended the cover-over through the 2008 and 2009 tax years. In the 111th Congress, the Tax Relief, Unemployment Insurance Reauthorization, and Job Creation Act of 2010 (P.L. 111-312) extended the cover-over at $13.25 through 2011. The legislation was signed by the President on December 17, 2010, thus, the additional covered-over revenue will be remitted retroactively at the higher rate.

In the 112th Congress, legislation has been introduced to expand federal control over the use of covered-over revenue. Passage of H.R. 1883 (or similar legislation, S. 986) would result in limits on Puerto Rico's and the USVI's ability to use covered-over revenue to subsidize the rum industry in the islands. The legislation is likely in response to the recent economic development initiatives in the USVI financed in part by rum cover-over revenue. The President's FY2013 budget proposal includes an extension of the $13.25 cover-over, as does S. 3521. The U.S. Department of the Treasury (Treasury) collects federal excise tax revenue on rum exported to the United States from PR and the USVI and submits monthly reports of the amount collected to the U.S. Department of the Interior (DOI). In September, PR and the USVI request prepayment from the DOI based on revenue projections by the Office of Management and Budget (OMB) for the upcoming fiscal year. The DOI then requests that the Treasury deposit the funds by September 30 into a designated escrow account for PR and the USVI.

Table 1. Cover-Over Revenue for Puerto Rico and the U.S. Virgin Islands (FY1994 to FY2011, certified amounts in millions)

Fiscal	Grand	Virgin Islands			Puerto Rico		
Year	Total	Domestic	Other	Total	Domestic	Other	Total
1994	$235.3	$ 30.3	$2.6	$ 32.9	$184.8	$ 17.6	$202.4
1995	$249.2	$ 41.0	$2.0	$ 43.0	$193.9	$ 12.4	$206.2
1996	$263.8	$ 42.7	$2.3	$ 45.0	$202.0	$ 16.8	$218.8
1997	$268.0	$ 45.6	$2.5	$ 48.1	$203.1	$ 16.8	$219.9
1998	$262.8	$ 50.3	$2.3	$ 52.6	$194.1	$ 16.1	$210.2
1999	$296.8	$ 51.1	$2.8	$ 53.9	$223.9	$ 19.0	$242.9
2000	$363.7	$ 62.7	$3.0	$ 65.7	$275.1	$ 23.0	$298.1
2001	$408.2	$ 68.1	$3.5	$ 71.6	$311.9	$ 24.7	$336.6
2002	$409.8	$ 60.3	$5.1	$ 65.5	$304.7	$ 39.5	$344.3
2003	$430.5	$ 64.1	$6.4	$ 70.5	$314.1	$ 46.0	$360.0
2004	$421.5	$ 75.0	$6.2	$ 81.2	$300.9	$ 39.4	$340.3
2005	$476.1	$ 75.1	$6.0	$ 81.1	$345.7	$ 49.3	$395.0
2006	$433.0	$ 70.9	$6.5	$ 77.4	$316.2	$ 39.4	$355.6
2007	$552.7	$ 86.7	$8.1	$ 94.8	$399.7	$ 58.2	$457.9
2008	$510.6	$ 91.9	$7.6	$ 99.6	$353.4	$ 57.7	$411.1
2009	$547.1	$106.8	$8.6	$115.4	$368.9	$ 62.8	$431.7
2010	$482.0	$103.7	$8.9	$112.5	$311.4	$58.1	$369.5
2011*	$582.6	$123.9	$9.6	$133.5	n/a	n/a	$449.1
Total	$7,193.7	$1,250.2	$94.0	$1,344.3	$4,803.8	$ 596.8	$5,849.6

Source: Data are from e-mail correspondence with Carol Coy and Thomas Hogue from the U.S. Department of the Treasury, TTB, and Charlene Leizear from the U.S. Department of the Interior, Office of Insular Affairs.

Notes: The USVI cover-over is paid by the Trade and Tax Bureau of the U.S. Department of the Treasury and the U.S. Department of the Interior. The amount of the cover-over collected per proof gallon was $10.50 from FY1990 through FY1994, $11.30 from FY1995 to FY1998, $10.50 in FY1999 and FY2010, and $13.25 for FY2000 through FY2009. *The 2011 data for domestic and other rum for Puerto Rico was not available, but the total was provided by Carol Coy.

Cover-Over Revenue

In FY2011, PR received $449.1 million in covered-over revenue from domestic production and other country imports into the United States, combined. The USVI received $123.9 million from domestic production and $9.6 million from other country imports.[17] The "other country" import is the amount that is split between the USVI and PR based on market share. The

FY2010 split was roughly 13% to the USVI and 87% to PR. Table 1 reports the amount covered over to PR and USVI for each fiscal year since 1994. Since 1994, PR has received $5.8 billion and the USVI $1.3 billion. The U.S. Alcohol and Tobacco Tax and Trade Bureau (TTB) remits the entire cover-over to PR, which includes the tax collected on PR-sourced production and the PR share of the "other" revenue from U.S. imports from non-PR and non-USVI sources. In contrast, the cover-over for taxes collected on U.S. imports from the USVI is remitted by the DOI based on data provided by the TTB. The share of "other" revenue is remitted by the TTB.[18]

The Use of Cover-Over Revenue

Puerto Rico uses cover-over revenue to finance marketing and promotional activities for the rum industries. The exact amounts and extent of these activities is unclear as there is not separate publicly available budget accounting. However, a letter from Puerto Rico Resident Commissioner Pierluisi (and three other Members of Congress) states, "Puerto Rico currently uses a small fraction of its annual federal excise tax revenue—about 6%—to promote Puerto Rican rums in general."[19] The remaining 94% would be available for general expenditures in Puerto Rico, perhaps some of which could benefit the rum industry.

The USVI uses several tools to subsidize the production of rum in the USVI.[20] The Virgin Islands Public Finance Authority (VIPFA) issues tax-exempt bonds whose proceeds are used to finance public infrastructure spending, such as schools and roads, and infrastructure used almost exclusively by the rum industry. The size of the subsidy for the rum industry through state-sponsored debt finance is not transparent or easily measured. Debt for public infrastructure indirectly helps the rum industry and is not typically considered an industrial subsidy. The debt used for rum manufacturing infrastructure is direct, though measuring the subsidy is still problematic. Quantifying the subsidy requires establishing what costs, including taxes and fees, the industry would have incurred without the public assistance through tax favored debt.

Recently, the VIPFA has issued a series of bonds backed by the rum tax. These bonds are often referred to as "rum-tax bonds." In July 2008, according to a press report, the legislature of the USVI voted 10-5 in favor of a 30-year contractual agreement with Diageo, the maker of the Captain Morgan® brand rum among other beverages, to begin operations in the USVI (Diageo had contracted with a Puerto Rican based distiller to produce Captain Morgan®) and remain there for at least 30 years.[21] Since that agreement, the VIPFA has moved forward issuing so-called "rum-tax bonds" that are secured by cover-over revenues. There were three bond issues from the VIPFA backed by rum-tax revenues in 2009.

On July 9, 2009, the VIPFA offered $250 million of rum-tax bonds that would be subordinate to the agency's outstanding $477.8 million of senior rum-tax bonds.[22] The new issue will be used to "make a loan to the Government to provide a grant to Diageo USVI to finance the acquisition, design, construction, development and equipping of a rum production and maturation warehouse facility, and any improvements thereto, to be located on St. Croix."[23] According to the bond offering statement, these new bonds will create $12.2 million in annual debt service costs in 2010, $16.7 million from 2011 to 2013, and $20.6 million from 2014 through 2038.

On October 1, 2009, the VIPFA offered another $458,849,000 in bonds of which $363,840,000 was for the refunding of outstanding debt (rum-tax bonds that had been issued in 1998) and the remaining $95 million was for new money. The rum-tax bond new money ($95 million) was for capital projects including "school construction, water and sewer upgrades, building and road renovations, open space initiatives, and land acquisitions for affordable housing programs among other projects."[24]

On October 8, 2009, the VIPFA was reported to have plans to issue $105 million of rum bonds for a second rum maker, Cruzan. In return, Cruzan would agree to remain in the USVI for 30 years. The report indicates that $30 million of the bond issue would finance a new wastewater treatment facility and $75 million would help expand the Cruzan distillery.[25] On December 8, 2009, the VIPFA offered $39.2 million in bond finance for the Cruzan project.[26]

On July 8, 2010, the VIPFA offered $399,050,000 of bonds to then loan to the USVI government. The USVI government planned to use the loan proceeds to finance the capital reserve accounts needed for the various capital projects in process on the island.

The USVI Subsidy for Rum Production

There will be two principal rum producers operating in the USVI by 2012 and both will be receiving subsidies from the USVI government.

Cruzan, which is already producing rum, and Diageo, which is scheduled to begin production in 2012. In FY2009, Cruzan produced approximately 9.6 million proof gallons of Cruzan rum, of which 8 million proof gallons were sold in the United States.[27]

The Diageo production targets are included in the Diageo Agreement along with the USVI subsidy structure. The legislation signed by USVI Governor deJongh formalizing the agreement with Diageo USVI, Inc., included the following list of statutory incentives the government of the USVI is already providing to support rum production and has expanded to attract Diageo USVI, Inc.:

a. A Molasses Subsidy Fund to assist distillers engaged in the processing of molasses into rum within the Virgin Islands (33 V.I.C. §3036);
b. Statutorily provided marketing support payments designed to support the long-term growth of branded rum products to build a stable long-term rum industry;
c. Statutory exemptions on property, excise, gross receipts and income taxes and other local tax incentives; and
d. Environmental mitigation support.

In the documents accompanying the December 8, 2009, bond issue, the VIPFA listed three sources of subsidy and support for Cruzan rum production: (1) a molasses subsidy payment; (2) a marketing support agreement with a termination of November 21, 2011; and (3) a professional services agreement with Cruzan entered into on June 23, 2006, extended annually and was set to expire on December 31, 2009 (as of this writing, the status of this agreement is uncertain).

Table 2 lists the support of Cruzan rum from fiscal years 2003 through 2009. In the most recent year listed, the USVI provided direct support of $21.3 million for Cruzan rum.

This represents roughly 18.5% of the amount received in covered-over revenue from the excise tax on rum imported from the USVI. The most recent bond offering statement included estimates for FY2010 for the Cruzan rum promotion and marketing support payments in the amount of $22,709,948 and $12,913,059.[28]

Table 2. USVI Subsidies for Cruzan Rum, FY2003 Through FY2009

Fiscal Year	Rum Promotion	Marketing Support	Molasses Subsidy	Total
2003	$1,358,684	$ -	$ 3,477,651	$4,836,335
2004	$2,246,601	$ -	$ 4,000,000	$6,246,601
2005	$1,982,402	$ -	$ 4,400,000	$6,382,402
2006	$2,412,691	$ -	$ 6,900,000	$9,312,691
2007	$1,467,769	$1,920,980	$8,373,642	$11,762,390
2008	$1,487,248	$694,466a	$11,678,678	$13,860,391
2009	$2,144,461	$3,878,110	$15,312,338	$21,334,909

Source: USVI Office of Management and Budget as reported in the VIPFA Bond Offering Statement of December 8, 2009, cited earlier, pp. 50-51.

a. The marketing support payments for FY2008 are low because an invoice was late and was billed in FY2009.

RECENT LEGISLATIVE ACTIVITY

On May 12, 2011, Resident Commissioner Pedro Pierluisi introduced H.R. 1883, the Investing in U.S. Territories, Not Corporations Act of 2011, legislation that would limit the amount of the subsidy to rum companies that is paid with covered-over revenue. In addition, the legislation would restrict the allocation of the covered-over revenue.

The subsidy limit would prevent any possession from offering more than 15% of their covered-over revenue as an industrial subsidy for the rum industry. The restriction seems intended to make it more costly for the USVI to provide incentives to rum producers that have relocated from Puerto Rico to the USVI.[29] Resident Commissioner Pierluisi, in a news item that appeared on his congressional website, states that

> Using funds provided under the federal cover-over program to give excessive subsidies to companies is completely indefensible. It destroys the purpose and integrity of this important program, which was intended to help the territories provide essential government services, like health care, infrastructure development, education, and land conservation....[30]

The legislation would allow the possessions to offer debt financed grants to rum producers in excess of the 15% limit as long as the debt were not repaid with cover-over revenues. Thus, any amount of cover-over revenue used to repay debt that was issued to subsidize rum producers would be included in the 15% limit. The amount above the 15% limit would be subtracted from the cover-over payment for the next two years. In the Senate, S. 986, introduced by Senator Menendez, includes the same provisions.

A second provision in the proposed bills would restrict the allocations of rum cover-over revenue to the USVI and Puerto Rico. Puerto Rico's share of the cover-over revenue could never fall below 65% or rise above 70%. The USVI share would then be bound between 30% and 35%. Under current law, there is no limit on the cover-over revenue generated by own-source rum exports. In 2009, roughly 88% of all cover-over revenue was returned to Puerto Rico as Diageo produced Captain Morgan® rum in Puerto Rico. The recent relocation of Diageo operations from Puerto Rico to the USVI is anticipated to shift the relative market share significantly. The 35% cap on USVI remittances, as proposed, would likely be significantly lower than actual market share. A recent bond offering statement included an estimate that total cover-over revenues to the USVI would increase from to $278.8 million in 2013.[31] The increase, due largely from new Diageo rum shipments, would likely mirror a decrease in Puerto Rican shipments.[32]

S. 3521 would extend the higher cover-over amount of $13.25 without any modifications to the allocation or restrictions on use of revenues.

Potential Impact

H.R. 1883 and S. 986 would make the direct subsidy to rum producers with rum excise tax cover-over payments more difficult and preclude the USVI from using general revenue to subsidize rum producers. As identified earlier, the subsidy the USVI is offering would include the continuation of (1) rum promotion, (2) marketing support, and (3) a molasses subsidy.[33] In addition, news reports have also suggested that the USVI would provide income tax breaks and a complete exemption from property taxes. The news report also claims that the sum of these subsidies approaches 46% of the total amount covered over to the USVI and is not directly linked to the rum cover-over.[34]

All of these benefits accompany the debt finance support outlined earlier. The so-called rum-tax bonds are clearly linked to the rum tax as they are secured by the revenue generated by the production and export of Captain Morgan® by Diageo. The mix of marketing subsidies and tax incentives used to attract Diageo to the USVI already exceeds the limits proposed in the legislation. What is unclear is how the legislation would affect the Diageo agreement, enacted in July 2008, to manufacture rum in the USVI. Section 6.2.1(b) on page 23 of the Diageo agreement stipulates that Diageo will produce rum in the USVI as long as "the Economic Development incentives granted by the Government to Diageo have not been materially reduced or made unavailable to Diageo." The restrictions that would be imposed on the cover-over revenues would likely reduce the subsidies provided by the USVI to Diageo. It is unclear how Diageo would respond to enactment of the legislation.

Analysis

Supporters of the restrictions claim that the tax incentives and subsidies offered by the USVI to large profitable corporations, such as Diageo, are a misuse of taxpayer dollars. Others make the same argument against many government-funded sub-federal economic development incentives. Some researchers "have begun to write off economic development incentives as ineffective or inefficient for a host of reasons."[35]

Nevertheless, the justification for using tax incentives and subsidies to attract industry has long been a part of non-federal economic development strategies. There are numerous examples of states offering manufacturing firms reduced property taxes, access to tax-exempt financing, and favorable corporate income tax policies. The success of these programs to retain or lure new firms has been mixed and in many cases critics assert that the programs unnecessarily sacrifice tax revenues to influence a location decision that has already been made.

From the federal government's perspective, state and local incentives for industrial development are a redistribution of tax dollars from state and local governments to manufacturing firms without a net gain in national GDP. From this perspective, the incentives shift economic activity from one location in the United States to another. The intended improvement of social welfare (i.e., helping economically disadvantaged areas) is usually the justification for such policies in light of what many economists identify as the "zero-sum" nature of the incentives.

The size and scope of the USVI agreement with Diageo (and, to a lesser degree, Cruzan) is unique in that it involves the cover-over of rum excise tax revenues from the U.S. Departments of the Treasury and the Interior to the USVI and PR to directly and indirectly support the rum industry. The legislation would not prohibit tax incentives and direct subsidies; just limit them to a seemingly arbitrary level.

The proposed limit could also be seen as inconsistent with the intent of the cover-over as expressed in the legislation and report language cited earlier. As noted in the legislative history in this report, Congress explicitly stated that the government receiving the covered-over revenue was charged with its disposition, not the U.S. Congress.

In the case of Diageo, news reports indicate that Diageo had already decided to leave Puerto Rico and the USVI presented the most attractive option. While other Caribbean countries were said to be in the competition for the Diageo facility, Diageo's decision to produce rum in the USVI presents the worst case scenario for PR because PR loses not only Diageo but also future excise tax revenue from USVI production. As mentioned previously, a portion of rum-tax revenue collected from other countries' imports to the United States is paid to PR, but not on imports from the USVI.

The recent recession and related budget situation have elevated the interest in the rum cover-over program.[36] From the perspective of U.S. taxpayers, some may question the efficacy of the rum cover-over, regardless of the historical precedent. Further, proponents of restrictions on the use of covered-over revenue have alluded to the possibility that Congress may reconsider the cover-over principle generally, possibly ending the program, if the USVI uses the revenue for "unreasonable" subsidies.

APPENDIX. CONGRESSIONAL HEARINGS ON THE RUM COVER-OVER

U.S. Congress, House Committee on Ways and Means, Subcommittee on Select Revenue Measures, *Miscellaneous Tax Bills*, 99th Cong., 1st sess., May 12 and 19, 1986.

- Hearing includes consideration of H.R. 4578, to require the Unite States to pay to the Virgin Islands the full amount of excise taxes imposed on rum produced in the Virgin Islands.

U.S. Congress, House Committee on Ways and Means, *Tax Shelters, Accounting Abuses, and Corporate and Securities Reforms*, 98th Cong., 2nd sess., February 22 and 28, 1984.

- Hearing includes consideration of H.R. 4702, to disallow federal excise tax rebates to Puerto Rico and the Virgin Islands for redistilled spirits originally distilled in the U.S.

U.S. Congress, Senate Committee on Energy and Natural Resources, Subcommittee on Energy Conservation and Supply, *1983 Omnibus Territories*, 98th Cong., 1st sess., October 6, 1983.

- Hearing includes consideration of S. 589, to authorize FY1984 appropriations for certain Guam public works projects, and to authorize or revise various programs pertaining to Guam, NMI, and Virgin Islands. Includes provision to eliminate the federal approval requirement for Virgin Islands spending of rum excise tax rebates.

U.S. Congress, Senate Committee on Energy and Natural Resources, *Caribbean Basin Initiative*, 98th Cong., 1st sess., June 10, 1983.

- Hearing to examine the implications of President Reagan's February 1982 Caribbean Basin Initiative (CBI) for the Virgin Islands and Puerto Rico. Focuses on CBI provision to rebate rum excise tax revenue to the Virgin Islands and Puerto Rico to protect their economies from adverse CBI effects. Includes brief consideration of S. 544, the Caribbean Basin Economic Recovery Act, to authorize trade and tax incentives to encourage Caribbean area economic revitalization.

U.S. Congress, House Committee on Ways and Means, *Caribbean Basin Economic Recovery Act*, 98th Cong., 1st sess., June 9, 1983.

- Hearing to consider H.R. 2769, to authorize trade and tax incentives to encourage Caribbean area economic revitalization. Includes provisions to require Treasury Dept to transfer to Puerto Rico and the Virgin Islands excise tax revenues from all rum imported into the United States.

U.S. Congress, Senate Committee on Finance, *Caribbean Basin Initiative*, 98th Cong., 1st sess., April 13, 1983.

- Hearing to consider S. 544, the Caribbean Basin Economic Recovery Act (summary, p. 3-10), the Administration bill, to authorize trade and tax incentives to encourage Caribbean area economic revitalization, including duty-free treatment through September 30, 1995, of qualifying Caribbean products imported into the U.S. Includes witness statements on the potential adverse effect of S. 544 on Puerto Rico and U.S. Virgin Islands, particularly on local bulk rum industries and U.S. imported rum excise tax rebate revenues; presentation of Puerto Rico-Virgin Islands alternative to proposed duty-free treatment of rum.

U.S. Congress, Senate Committee on Finance, *Caribbean Basin Initiative*, 97th Cong., 2nd sess., August 2, 1982.

- Hearing to consider S. 2237, the Caribbean Basin Economic Recovery Act, to implement President Reagan's February 1982 Caribbean Basin Initiative (CBI) to promote economic revitalization in the Caribbean area and Central America through duty-free treatment of certain articles, increased economic assistance, and tax credit for U.S. capital investment in Caribbean Basin countries. Includes statement by the Puerto Rico Manufacturers Association on the impact of the act on the Puerto Rican rum industry.

U.S. Congress, Senate Committee on Foreign Relations, *Caribbean Basin Initiative*, 97th Cong., 2nd sess., March 25, 31, 1982.

- Hearings to consider S. 2237, to implement President Reagan's February 1982 Caribbean Basin Initiative (CBI) to encourage Caribbean area economic revitalization through duty-free treatment of certain articles, increased economic assistance, and tax credits for U.S. capital investments in Caribbean Basin countries. Includes discussion of concerns about impact of CBI duty-free provisions on competitive position of Virgin Islands industries, focusing on rum industry; views on overall U.S. policies and program priorities for Caribbean region.

U.S. Congress, House Committee on Ways and Means, Subcommittee on Trade, *Caribbean Basin Initiative*, 97th Cong., 2nd sess., March 17, 23-25, 1982.

- Hearings to consider H.R. 5900, to implement President Reagan's February 1982 Caribbean Basin Initiative (CBI) to encourage Caribbean area economic revitalization through duty-free treatment of certain articles, increased economic assistance, and tax credits for U.S. capital investment in Caribbean Basin countries. Also assesses CBI effects on Puerto Rico and the Virgin Islands, and includes discussion on concerns about foreseen anticompetitive effect on Virgin Islands rum industry of duty-free entry for all Caribbean rums.

U.S. Congress, House Committee on Ways and Means, Subcommittee on Trade, *Multilateral Trade Negotiations*, 96th Cong., 1st sess., April 23-27, 1979.

- Hearings to examine the advantages and disadvantages of the Multilateral Trade Negotiations (MTN) agreements for U.S. industries. Includes statements by representatives from Puerto Rico and the U.S. Virgin Islands on the importance of rum industry to represented islands' economic stability and development; impact of rum tariff reduction; objections to duty and excise taxes assessment based on proof content as opposed to current gallonage standards.

U.S. Congress, House Committee on Ways and Means, *Tax Remissions to Virgin Islands*, 80th Cong., 2nd sess., February 3, 18, 27, 1948.

- Hearings to consider S. 1014 and H.R. 4979, which provide that proceeds from Federal taxes imposed on articles produced in the Virgin Islands be made available to the territorial legislature.

U.S. Congress, House Committee on Insular Affairs, *To Assist in Relieving Economic Distress in Puerto Rico and the Virgin Islands, Part 4*, 78th Cong., 2nd sess., May 16-17, 1944.

- Hearing to consider H.R. 3777. Includes consideration of Virgin Islands civil works projects and rum industry tax allocations for public works programs.

U.S. Congress, House Committee on Insular Affairs, *To Assist in Relieving Economic Distress in the Virgin Islands. Part 3: Virgin Islands*, 78th

Cong., 1st sess., October 21, 27, November 2, 10, 17, and December 2, 6, 1943.

- Hearing includes discussion of proposals for Virgin Islands rum industry tax allocations for public works programs.

U.S. Congress, House Committee on Ways and Means, Subcommittee on Internal Revenue Taxation, *Appropriation of Certain Taxes to Virgin Islands*, 76th Cong., 1 sess., June 26-27, 1939.

- Hearing to consider S. 1685 and H.R. 4773. Involves the covering of taxes collected on articles of Virgin Islands manufacture into the treasury of the Virgin Islands.

End Notes

[1] Karla Hoff, "U.S. Federal Tax Policy Towards the Territories: Past, Present, and Future," *Tax Law Review* (Fall, 1981), p. 57.

[2] The rebates are paid by the U.S. Alcohol and Tobacco Tax and Trade Bureau (TTB) within the U.S. Treasury. According to data provided by that agency in the federal FY2009 budget, the payment to Puerto Rico in 2007 was $462 million.

[3] The Caribbean Basin Initiative reduced customs duties on imported rum. This introduced the possibility that sales in the U.S. of rum shipped from the possessions would fall, and so too would cover-overs to the possessions of federal excise taxes from rum manufactured in the possessions. The additional cover-overs were enacted to offset the expected loss of revenue. U.S. Congress, House, Committee on Ways and Means, *Caribbean Basin Economic Recovery Act*, H.Rept. 98-266, 98th Cong., 1st Sess. (Washington: GPO, 1983), p. 26.

[4] The Organic Act of 1954, however, did provide that "approval of the President or his designated representative shall be obtained before such moneys may be obligated or expended." The approval provision is no longer in 26 U.S.C. §7652.

[5] Data for Puerto Rico are from Carol Coy, U.S. Department of Treasury, Alcohol and Tobacco Tax and Trade Bureau. Data for the USVI are from the Virgin Island Public Finance, *Bond Offering Statement for Subordinated Revenue Bonds, Virgin Islands Matching Fund Loan Note—Cruzan Project*, December 9, 2009, p. 23.

[6] Jones Act of 1917, §9, 39 Stat. 951; 1910-1917.

[7] U.S. Congress, Committee on Insular Affairs, Report to Accompany H.R. 9533, *Civil Government for Porto Rico*, Report no. 77, 64th Congress, 1st sess., January 16, 1916, p. 2.

[8] Section 28(b) of P.L. 83-517, 68 Stat. 508.

[9] U.S. Congress, Senate Report to Accompany S. 3378, *Revision of the Organic Act of the Virgin Islands*, Report no. 1271, 83rd Congress, 2nd sess., April 29, 1954, p. 5.

[10] Ibid., p. 6.

[11] Information from the proposed legislation presented to the USVI legislature by Gov. DeJongh. Brugal is a rum maker based in the Dominican Republic and is no longer producing rum in the USVI. Cruzan is still operating in the USVI.

[12] CRS calculation based on data for FY2009 in Table 1 of this report.

[13] U.S. Congress, Committee on Ways and Means, Report to Accompany H.R. 2769, *The Caribbean Basin Economic Recovery Act*, 98th Congress, 1st session, Report no. 98-266, June 24, 1983, p. 27.

[14] For a complete description, see *Federal Register*, vol. 51, No. 150, August 5, 1986, pp. 28071-28078. Also, additional data are from a memorandum entitled "Virgin Islands and Puerto Rico Cover-over," from Kahau Morrison, ATF Office of Congressional Liason, U.S. Department of the Treasury to David Brumbaugh, Congressional Research Service, April 2, 2001, p. 5.

[15] A proof gallon is a combination of alcohol content and volume. A proof gallon is the volume in gallons, multiplied by the percent alcohol, multiplied by 2, and divided by 100.

[16] U.S. Congress, Joint Committee on Taxation, *General Explanation of the Revenue Provisions of the Deficit Reduction Act of 1984* (Washington: GPO, 1984), p. 1,226.

[17] Unlike for PR, the IRS does not have a USVI branch that collects the excise tax. Instead, the Customs Service within the DOI collects the excise tax on USVI imports.

[18] The reason for the DOI remittance is based on budgetary and administrative reasons.

[19] Letter from Resident Commissioner Pedro R. Pierluisi, Honorable Luis V. Gutierrez, Honorable José E. Serrano, and Honorable Nydia M. Velázquez to the Honorable Charles B. Rangel, November 10, 2009.

[20] News reports have indicated that Puerto Rico uses no more than 10% of covered-over rum tax revenue for the promotion of Puerto Rican rum in the United States. The Puerto Rico Industrial Development Corporation (PRIDCO) website did not provide detailed accounting for any industrial incentives explicitly for the rum industry or any information on the cover-over of rum taxes. The presumption is that the covered-over revenues are included in the general fund.

[21] Susan Mann, "USVI Governor Scores 10-5 Victory for Diageo," Caribbean Net News, July 12, 2008.

[22] Subordinate bonds are second in line to the revenue dedicated to the "senior" debt. This means the bonds are less secure than the senior debt.

[23] VIPFA bond offering statement document for $250 million of Subordinated Revenue Bonds, June 26, 2009.

[24] VIPFA bond offering statement, June 26, 2009.

[25] Michelle Kaske, "Virgin Islands Deal for Cruzan Rum," the *Bond Buyer*, October 8, 2009.

[26] VIPFA bond offering statement document for $39.2 million of Subordinated Revenue Bonds, December 8, 2009.

[27] VIPFA bond offering statement document for $399.050 million of Revenue Bonds, dated July 8, 2010, p. 41.

[28] Ibid., p. 43.

[29] The bond-offering statements identified earlier include mention of the legislation as one of the "risks" to bond holders implying if the legislation were to become law, the bonds would be at greater risk of default.

[30] The quote can be found at http://pierluisi.house.gov/english/news/2010/ 05.12.2011%20PRP%20protects%20rum.html.

[31] See VIPFA bond offering statement document for $399,050,000 of Revenue Bonds, July 8, 2010, p. 26.

[32] The USVI share would likely rise to over 50% of cover-over revenue in 2013 based on assumptions on USVI rum productions projections presented in the July 8, 2010 bond offering statement cited earlier. However, similar estimates on the expected impact on Puerto Rican rum exports are not available.

[33] Molasses is the key input for rum production.

[34] Marcus Stern, "Bailout Bill a Sweet Deal for Rum Maker," *Politico*, October 26, 2008.

[35] For a discussion of the criticisms and current views on state economic development incentives, see Dan Gorin, "Economic Development Incentives: Research Approaches and Current Views," *Federal Reserve Bulletin*, Federal Reserve Board, October 2008, pp. A61-A73; available at http://www.federalreserve.gov/pubs/bulletin/2008/articles/ econdevelopment /default.htm.

[36] Ryan J. Donmoyer, "Bailout of U.S. Banks Gives British Rum a $2.7 Billion Benefit," Bloomberg News, June 26, 2009, available at http://www.bloomberg.com/apps/news?pid= 20601109&sid=amp5wXx35fkc.

INDEX

D

E

F

G

H